Praise for *Your Church Is Too Small*

John Armstrong has spent his entire ministry working to build the church and has sometimes paid a dear price for insisting that true believers in every communion must work together to reassert the unity of Christ's body. This book is John's story and manifesto for the much-needed work of building bridges, forging alliances, and renewing oneness across all the various expressions of the church of Jesus Christ. It's a must-read for anyone who has grown weary of Christian divisiveness and schism and longs to discover ways of strengthening the bonds that unite us in the Spirit of Christ.

> —Chuck Colson, founder, Prison Fellowship and Chuck Colson Center for Christian Worldview

Every once in a while, I read a book I wish every Christian I know would read. This is that kind of book. *Your Church Is Too Small* is clear, prophetic, practical—and true. If you pray for reformation, renewal, and revival in America and the world (and I do daily), this book is the place to put legs on those prayers. You will be shocked, irritated, and stirred deeply—and then you'll rise up and call John Armstrong blessed for having had the courage and call to write it and me for having the wisdom to commend it to you.

> —Steve Brown, president and teacher, Key Life Network, Inc.

If the late Lesslie Newbigin could offer today's church an exhortation—a reminder from the past, an assessment of the present, and encouragement for the future—what would the old bishop say? In what he terms *missional-ecumenism*, John Armstrong proposes an answer that confronts readers with the universal shape of Christian identity.

> —Chris Castaldo, author of *Holy Ground: Walking with Jesus as a Former Catholic*

The apostle Paul wrote that maintaining the unity of the Spirit in the bond of peace among Jesus' followers is hard work (Ephesians 4:3). Few people know that better than John Armstrong. In a day when everything about the contemporary church militates against oneness, John is working to break down the walls we've built up so that the world can see Jesus in all his variegated richness, in the fullness of the one body of Christ. This book provides the blueprints and marching orders for a new generation of Church-builders (capital C) in all the communions of the body of Christ.

> —T.M. Moore, dean of the Centurions, Prison Fellowship

Your Church Is Too Small maps out the painful yet liberating trek from sectarian isolation to the spirit of orthodox unity. In opening oneself to fellow believers, there is no escaping the tension between purity and embrace. No one can sort out that puzzle this side of the second coming. But John Armstrong's book gives courage and strength for the journey. Read this book, take heart, and go forth.

> —David Neff, editor in chief and vice president, *Christianity Today*

A growing appreciation for catholicism—the whole church spread across the whole world—is one of the most hopeful signs emerging within recent evangelicalism. John Armstrong's astute, heartfelt book provides excellent guidance for the twenty-first-century evangelical rediscovery of the classical church and its rich tradition.

> —Rodney Clapp, author of *Tortured Wonders*

Protestant, Catholic, and Orthodox Christians who call Jesus Lord are obligated to fulfill his Great Commission and his "new command" to love one another. Our lack of visible unity and ecumenical charity hinders our mission. John Armstrong's *Your Church Is Too Small* is a humble, honest, and openhearted summons to "resize" our churches (and our hearts) by taking seriously the prayer Jesus prayed for us on the eve of his crucifixion. May this encouraging, provocative, and practical book not only be read widely but also be acted on out of love for the One who saves us all.

> —James M. Kushiner, executive editor, *Touchstone: A Journal of Mere Christianity*

JOHN H. ARMSTRONG

your church is too small

WHY UNITY IN CHRIST'S MISSION IS VITAL

TO THE FUTURE OF THE CHURCH

ZONDERVAN®

ZONDERVAN.com/
AUTHORTRACKER
follow your favorite authors

ZONDERVAN

Your Church Is Too Small
Copyright © 2010 by John H. Armstrong

This title is also available as a Zondervan ebook.
Visit www.zondervan.com/ebooks.

This title is also available in a Zondervan audio edition.
Visit www.zondervan.fm.

Requests for information should be addressed to:

Zondervan, *Grand Rapids, Michigan 49530*

Library of Congress Cataloging-in-Publication Data

Armstrong, John H. (John Harper), 1949-
    Your church is too small : why unity in Christ's mission is vital to the future of
the church / John Armstrong.
      p. cm.
    Includes bibliographical references.
    ISBN 978-0-310-32114-9 (hardcover, printed)
    1. Church — Unity. I. Title.
BV601.5.A76 2010
262'.72 — dc22   2009037496

Interior design: Matthew Van Zomeren
Cover design: Kirk DouPonce, DogEared Design

Printed in the United States of America

10 11 12 13 14 15 16 17 • 22 21 20 19 18 17 16 15 14 13 12 11 10 9 8 7 6 5 4 3 2 1

For the advancement of the missional mandate
of Jesus Christ in the third millennium
and the renewal of biblical ecumenism
through the witness of Holy Scriptures
and the wisdom of the Christian tradition.

And for my granddaughter, Abigail Faith Armstrong,
who has an amazing joy for life
and a passionate spirit like her grandfather.
Abbie, I pray that you will make
a real difference in the next generation
as you contribute your part
to the unity of the church
in fulfilling Christ's mission.

Contents

past
THE BIBLICAL AND HISTORICAL
BASIS FOR CHRISTIAN UNITY

present
RESTORING UNITY IN THE CHURCH TODAY

future
THE MISSIONAL-ECUMENICAL MOVEMENT

Acknowledgments

WINSTON CHURCHILL ONCE SAID that writing a book usually begins as an adventure, becomes a mistress, then a master, after that a tyrant, and finally, just before you are ready to come to peace with your chains, you "kill the monster and fling him to the public." I identify with Churchill's observation. I have authored or edited eleven previous books. Each had unique moments, good and bad. But none involved the deep joy—and profound trials—of this book. In a very real sense, this book is the result of more than ten years of reading, thinking, listening, learning, and writing. Though the opinions here are all mine and clearly subject to criticism, I believe that God helped me through those tough moments in a profound way.

There are scores of friends who helped make this book possible. You know who you are and how much I appreciate your love and support. Stacy Kifer, my daughter and personal administrative assistant, has relieved a number of day-to-day pressures from my life so I could write. Anita, my bride of thirty-nine years, never lost faith in me or the book. She has lived this story as I sought to follow the vision that God gave me nearly fifteen years ago. We have no regrets. We never believed anything more deeply than this: There is "one holy catholic and apostolic church." I am profoundly grateful that we share this vision together.

Soli Deo Gloria.

Foreword

MY FRIEND JOHN ARMSTRONG is a church leader who has traveled the distance from the separatist, sectarian fixity of fundamentalism to embrace the kingdom-centered vision of the church and the call issued by a number of Bible-based theologians and missiologists during the past half century.

What vision is this? It is the one that views the visible church as a single worldwide, Spirit-sustained community within which ongoing doctrinal and denominational divisions, though important, are secondary rather than primary. In this vision, the primary thing is the missional-ecumenical vocation and trajectory crystallized for us by our Lord Jesus Christ in his teaching and prayer and illustrated in a normative way by the Acts narrative and much of the reasoning of the apostolic letters.

Evangelicals have always urged that the church of God is already one in Christ but have typically related this fact only to the invisible church (that is, the church as God alone sees it). All too often, they have settled for division in the visible church (the church on earth, as we see it) as at least tolerable and at best healthy. The vision Armstrong offers, however, perceives by exegesis that the unity of Christians, which Jesus prayed that the world might see, is neither unanimity nor uniformity nor union (as he neatly puts it) but loving cooperation in life and mission, starting from wherever we are at the moment and fertilized and energized by the creedal and devotional wisdom of the past. Thus the internal unity of togetherness in Christ may become a credibility factor in the church's outreach, just as Jesus in John 17 prayed that it would.

Embracing this vision will mean that our ongoing inter- and intra-church debates will look, and feel, less like trench warfare, in which both sides are firmly dug in to defend the territory that each sees as its heritage, and more like emigrants' discussions on shipboard that are colored by the awareness that soon they will be confronted by new tasks in an environment not identical with what they knew before. There they will all need to pull together in every way they can. The church in every generation voyages through historical developments and cultural changes, against the background of which new angles emerge on old debates and truths may need to be reformulated in order to remain truly the same as they were. Not to recognize this is a defect of vision on our part.

This perception, not surprisingly perhaps, disturbs persons brought up to believe that Bible-based doctrinal faithfulness counts supremely (yes, indeed, right so far), and that some form of ahistorical fundamentalist fixity was, is, and always will be the doctrinal last word. John Armstrong knows; he has been there. His corrected and corrective vision generates deep suspicion and an onslaught against its proponents as confused compromisers. Both he and I have learned this by direct experience. Some years ago, in *One Lord, One Faith*, Rex Koivisto made many of John Armstrong's points and was effectively ignored. I hope this book will not be ignored but will have the influence it deserves. Aspects of North America's future—aspects, indeed, of the honor and glory of Christ in this century—may well depend on whether or not it does.

—J. I. Packer, Advent 2009

Introduction

We are worthy of being believed only as we [are] aware of our unworthiness.
Karl Barth

All theology is biography.
Frederick Buechner

DO NOT ALLOW THE TITLE OF THIS BOOK to mislead you. I freely admit I borrowed the idea from J. B. Phillips's classic book *Your God Is Too Small*. By saying your church is too small, I am not referring to the physical size of a church building or to the number of people who attend services in your church building. I am referring to our all too common penchant for placing limits on Christ's church—limits that equate the one church with our own narrow views of Christ's body. When our church is too small, we adopt a desperately flawed image. The image shrivels our spirit and hinders Christ's mission. Please understand that the "small church" I refer to is a mind-set in believers that hinders the work of the Holy Spirit in mission and is contrary to the prayer of Jesus for our unity.

I would love to write a novel. Maybe someday I will. This book is definitely not a novel, but it *is* a story—my story. This is a journey of discovery, a journey to a great truth God began to teach me more about almost two decades ago. We all have a story with spiritual roots. I pray you will see yourself in my story. I have two purposes in telling it. First, I want you to understand your own spiritual identity in an entirely new way. Second, I want you to understand the mission of Christ in a manner that will grip your imagination and move you to pray and work for the renewal of the entire Christian church. More specifically, I hope you will gain a whole new understanding of what it means to be in the "one holy catholic and apostolic church."

I have come to believe, in the context of an ever-growing post-denominationalism in an emerging post-Christendom culture, that significant numbers of us are discovering how we share a common ancient faith that is greater than all of our historical and personal differences. C. S. Lewis appropriately called this faith "mere Christianity." This discovery will not pit the Bible against Christian **tradition**.* In fact, I will show how your biblical faith is rooted in the *living* Christian tradition, a tradition found in all the classical historical expressions of the one faith. This one faith is developing in ways we would have never thought possible while we were still indulging in the cultural luxury of seeing other Christians as our enemies. Many of us have begun to drink deeply from the wells of various Christian traditions.

I will argue that these unfolding developments may ultimately prevail in leading us to reject the conflicts and schisms that drove us apart and that these developments could result in a new commitment to the mission of Christ that will transform the church, especially in America.

I have been sensing a growing hunger for the renewal of Christian unity and mission for several decades, and I am convinced that what I have seen is not ephemeral. And so now I am attempting a serious vision recasting in this book. I hope you will agree with me and join a growing movement of people living out the ancient story in a modern context. I have dared to pray, as a friend taught me several years ago: *Dream a dream so big that it is destined to fail unless God is in it!*

---

* A glossary is provided in the back of this book with definitions of important terms. The first instance of each term found in the glossary is set in bold in the text.

past

THE BIBLICAL AND HISTORICAL BASIS FOR CHRISTIAN UNITY

chapter one

The Road to the Future

You can best think about the future of the faith after you have gone back to the classical tradition.

Robert E. Webber

When all is said (and truly said) about the divisions of Christendom, there remains, by God's mercy, an enormous common ground.

C. S. Lewis

No one dare do contemporary theology until they have mastered classical Christian thought.

Karl Barth

THE CHURCH TODAY IS MOVING through a significant time of transition. Some Christians have referred to this as a second Reformation or perhaps a fourth Great Awakening. What we know for sure is that cultural megashifts are rapidly occurring as globalization becomes more than simply an economic reality.

THE PAST CAN LEAD US TO THE FUTURE

New patterns of Christian faith and life are emerging in the church. I welcome these patterns, but I believe they desperately need to be rooted in the past—the creeds, the Word of God understood as the story of grace, life as a sacramental mystery, and deeply rooted **spiritual formation**. My thesis is simple: *The road to the future must run through the past.* My friend, the late Robert

Webber, called it "ancient-future faith." I share his perspective because the church must be rooted in the past and the future.

The incarnation of Jesus Christ in human history is *our* story. All Christians are spiritually united with the glorified Christ through the gift of the Holy Spirit. This results in a collective story that we live together in the present—yet also a story that has been powerfully shaped by the historical events and traditions of nearly two thousand years. Our modern story confuses us at times. The church gives mixed signals. Our historical past sometimes embarrasses us, especially if we know our profound inconsistencies. Nevertheless, as people of faith this is "our" story. Why?

True Christian faith is not found in personal religious feelings but in the historical and incarnational reality of a confessing church. Therefore, if we refuse to come to grips with our past, our future will not be distinctively Christian. The result will be new forms of man-made religion that embrace recycled heresies.

For almost two thousand years, Christians have lived the mystery of the apostolic faith and passed it on through personal stories, sermons, creeds, and common practices. But American Christians have a unique predilection to approach the Christian faith as if what we know is vastly more relevant than what previous generations knew. To do so is naive at best and dangerous at worst. It has led a generation of Christians to assume that they know perfectly well who Jesus is, apart from any instruction in ancient Christian tradition. America has, in fact, become a breeding ground for new religions and **sects**. Now we export these to Africa, Asia, and Latin America, which results in thousands of new denominations and splinter groups and an unimaginable number of cults. Something about all this tribalism rightly disturbs younger Christians.

Building one's faith and life on various passages in the Bible understood through private experience results in nothing less than a confusing cacophony of Christian noise. This situation is precisely what this book will challenge. I will make a case for how the one church of Jesus Christ, ministering out of its spiritual unity in Christ and rooted in core **orthodoxy**, can best serve Christ's mission.

SCRIPTURE IS GOD'S
SUPREME WITNESS TO CHRIST

My foundational premise is that Scripture bears the supreme witness to the living Christ, the final revelation of God. Christ has promised to build his church (Matthew 16:18). The visible church must be rooted in Scripture. But the great traditions of historical, incarnational, and confessional Christianity all flow from Scripture and the life of the church. Scripture alone, without human life and community consensus, is subject to every human whim and fancy. History demonstrates the danger of such an approach.

We must learn to listen to the witness of the whole church through Scripture. The Scriptures are "the word of God [and thus] alive and active. Sharper than any double-edged sword, it penetrates ..." (Hebrews 4:12). The Scriptures illumine the minds of God's people in every culture and context. By them, we freshly perceive truth as the Holy Spirit reveals Christ. The whole church comes to know God's wisdom and character through the Holy Scriptures. Christians believe that Scripture is perfect in all it affirms and authoritative for all people and cultures.

But the Christian church is flawed, sometimes profoundly so. After all, the church is a worldwide fellowship of human persons with all their personal and collective flaws. But we remain Christ's church. He promised to build his church, and he has kept his promise—a promise he will continue to keep until he comes again.

THE CHURCH: UNIFIED AND DIVERSE

During the first 1,800 years of Christian history almost no one understood the church as a myriad of independent and unrelated congregations and movements that interpreted the Bible as each saw fit. Even the sixteenth-century Protestant Reformers, especially magisterial men like Martin Luther and John Calvin, understood that there was an established historical foundation deeply rooted in the Scripture. The creeds and the doctrines taught by a consensus of the early church fathers were continually appealed to by all the great Protestant Reformers. For them, common faith was expressed in the earliest **ecumenical** creeds. The Reformers never encouraged people to pick through the Bible and concoct a better version of Christianity.

Growing evidence indicates the church is coming together in a new expression of unity and diversity. This is happening through the work of the Holy Spirit, reminding us that the church is the creation of God. This new expression is shaped by mission and **ecumenism**.

HOW THE AMERICAN MEGASHIFT WENT BAD

I have no doubt that the church in the West will undergo significant shifts in the coming decades, shifts that are already underway and incline some to radically rethink the church. The outcome could be widespread confusion. A diluted understanding of the once-and-for-all nature of faith could lead many to change virtually everything about the nature and form of the church. There are scores of books that take this approach, arguing intensely that the postmodern condition requires a complete revolt against historic Christianity. I see a much better solution.

Much rethinking about the church is confused precisely because it seeks an ideal church while denying the actual reality of the historical church. I advocate what is often called **critical realism**, which involves a positive yet critical response to the past and allows the past to be properly linked with a biblically hopeful view about what God will do in the age to come. My critical realism is rooted in several places: the study of Scripture, the story of the historical church, the foundation laid down by the earliest Christian leaders in the ecumenical creeds, and the various movements of the Holy Spirit that have renewed the church through the years. The Christian church is not a perfect community but is comprised of a redeemed people called to continual repentance in the gospel.

As a community, we must embody the gospel for the sake of the world. Having done this imperfectly in the past is never an excuse that should hinder us from praying for God to grant us more grace-given reality. Critical-realism holds before us the priority of the kingdom of God and the commitment of Christ himself to complete the work he began with his disciples and now carries on through us (see John 17).

The final book in the Bible makes plain what God will do before this present age ends. John was given a picture of Jesus and his throne in heaven and then wrote,

> You are worthy to take the scroll
>   and to open its seals,
> because you were slain,
>   and with your blood you purchased for God
>   members of every tribe and language
>   and people and nation.
> You have made them to be a kingdom and priests
>   to serve our God,
>   and they will reign on the earth.
>
> *Revelation 5:9 – 10*

This theme of the Lamb redeeming men and women from every tribe, language, people, and nation has driven the modern mission movement, now reaching a profound crescendo in the third millennium. East and West, North and South, the **missional** theme of the Bible has begun to transform Christians of all persuasions. This theme is one of victory. I believe the unity of the church will play a huge role in how this transformation transpires. This is why I argue that the future of the church is vitally connected to our unity in Christ's mission.

Specifically, I urge you to rethink the nature of the church, not its programmatic performance or persistent differences. American Christians talk a great deal about megashifts, which has led us to evaluate the performance of the church endlessly. In the process, multitudes of pragmatists have made the church a proverbial wax nose shaped by the newest book or seminar on trends and techniques. This approach is often based on polls, ministry/ spiritual gift inventories, and various theories rooted in marketing. A major development within many local congregations is to write mission/vision statements. We are right to be weary of many of these approaches since they sap our collective soul dry and fail to give us a big vision of what God intends to do throughout the world.

I am not pessimistic about the long-range direction of the church for one simple reason: *It belongs to Christ*. Congregations flourish where the kingdom of God breaks out. The church will accomplish God's purpose because Christ has won the victory. He will expand his kingdom to every nation and corner of the globe. He said so. We live between two ages—in what has been rightly called "the already/not yet." We live between the initial coming of Christ and his final appearing, when he will put down the last rebellion against his kingdom. So the church will yet play the decisive role in the great worldwide developments of history. What the church might look like, in terms of cultural forms, is anybody's guess. Futurists have a field day selling ideas about what this will be. In the end, we simply do not know.

WHAT IS GOD REALLY DOING IN OUR TIME?

The Spirit seems to be taking us through a worldwide transition period in which the prayer of Jesus in John 17:20–24 is being answered in previously unheard-of ways. While earlier movements for a unified church failed, some elements are now gaining new expression, especially among evangelicals and Roman Catholics. This development particularly interests me. *Where is the church actually discovering oneness, and how is it preparing the world to receive the gospel of the kingdom?* We must not grow weary but remember that God can accomplish in one day what we think should take years or even centuries. When it comes to the movement of the Spirit to restore our biblical unity, I ask, "Is anything too hard for the Lord?" (Genesis 18:14).

In trying to take the pulse of Christians and churches through reading, listening, traveling, and teaching, I have seen something of the heart of God's people. In America, massive change is not yet happening. But there is a fresh and serious searching, particularly among young people. In her book *The New Faithful*, Colleen Carroll raises provocative questions:

> Why are young adults who have grown up in a society saturated with relativism—which declares that ethical and religious truths vary according to the people who hold them—touting the truth claims of Christianity with such confidence? Why, in a society brimming with competing be-

lief systems and novel spiritual trends, are young adults attracted to the trappings of tradition that so many of their parents and professors have rejected? Is this simply the reaction of a few throwbacks to a bygone era, a few scattered inheritors of a faith they never critically examined? Is it the erratic behavior of young idealists moving through an inevitably finite religious phase? Or are they the heralds of something new? Could these young adults be proof that the demise of America's Judeo-Christian tradition has been greatly exaggerated?[1]

I am convinced that some Christians, and a growing number of congregations, are experiencing something previously unknown in American church history: Catholics and Protestants are learning to interact with one another in gracious ways. They are forming friendships not possible before. Even within the Eastern Orthodox Church, a church that very few Americans understand, similar relationships are forming, though on a vastly smaller scale. Thus there are people in all three of the great Christian traditions who are actually learning how to love one another. They are finding out that what unites them is much greater than what divides them. I believe this has to be the work of God's Spirit.

No matter what can be said about failed plans for unity under older forms of ecumenism, it cannot be said that these new developments are the work of the Enemy. It is not his way to lead us into genuine love for one another. In embracing our common roots in Trinitarian **orthodox** confession, we are beginning to experience the reality that there is "one body and one Spirit ... [and] one Lord, one faith, one baptism; one God and Father of all, who is over all and through all and in all" (Ephesians 4:4–6).

EVANGELICALS LEAVING THE CHURCH IN RECORD NUMBERS

At the same time I have hope for the recovery of Christian unity I see reports that evangelicals are quitting the church in record numbers. Julia Duin, a religion reporter for *The Washington Times*, wrote a book that provides mortifying evidence. She says that leaving is epidemic and concludes that "something is not right with church life, especially with evangelical church life."[2] I believe she is partially right.

The reasons for this exodus are numerous—loneliness, boredom, lack of community, church teaching that fails to go into the important truths of the faith, and the inability of the church to reach people who are suffering or going through deep trials, and more. Duin adds that a growing number of pastors are out of touch with their congregations and that their inefficient leadership models are failing the church. I see this problem every week. It is also not surprising to discover that women are leaving evangelical churches in larger numbers than men. Ms. Duin, a seminary graduate, says she was "one of those unwanted women for years."[3]

DISCOVERING OUR CHRISTIAN ROOTS

In 1976, author Alex Haley published a popular book titled *Roots: The Saga of an American Family*. His novel was adapted into a hugely popular twelve-hour television miniseries called *Roots*. Haley, an African-American, was reared on the stories of his elderly female relatives—including his grandmother Cynthia, an emancipated slave. With great stylistic freedom, the novel traces Haley's family history to *"the* African," a man named Kunta Kinte, captured by slave traders in 1767. According to Haley, generations of Kinte's enslaved descendants passed down their experiences orally. Haley researched African village customs, the slave trade, and the history of African-Americans in the United States. Not surprisingly, African-Americans were especially moved by the television series. It gave them a sense of their identity and of how they came to America. It took them back and then gave them hope for a better future, just as discovering our roots will move us forward to new faith, fresh hope, and genuine love.

Christians in America have lost a deep sense of their past, of their collective spiritual roots. As a result, we now suffer from a kind of spiritual amnesia that hinders our ability to faithfully move into the future with hope. This great loss overwhelms the radical optimism we need to make a lasting difference in the coming generation, a generation that will need a new sense of identity all the more if it is to thrive in a post-Christian culture.

QUESTIONS FOR
DISCUSSION AND REFLECTION

1. Why is understanding the past so important to the present and the future of the church? What happens when we ignore the past and plunge into a vision of the future?

2. Do you think the American church has become preoccupied with various methods for building the church rather than with worshiping the Christ who builds his own church? Why or why not?

3. Do you personally know Christians who are leaving the church or have already left? Why did they leave? What can be done about this problem?

4. What is meant by the phrase *small church* in this book?

chapter two

My Journey to Catholicity Begins

Whoever tears asunder the Church of God, disunites himself from Christ, who is the head, and who would have all his members to be united together.

John Calvin

Where Jesus Christ is, there also is the Catholic Church.

Ignatius of Antioch

IT WAS AN ORDINARY SUNDAY MORNING worship service. We were reciting the words of the Apostles' Creed, words I had said hundreds of times before. I knew the words. I believed them. But I had never been particularly moved by them. They were just words recited in a service.

But on this Sunday things unfolded very differently. As I said the words "I believe in the holy catholic church" from the Apostles' Creed, something stopped me. At that moment, the Holy Spirit spoke to my heart: "Do you *really* believe these words? If you believe them, then why don't you act like it?" The conviction was powerful and true. I was so shaken that I had to sit down. I wept. Questions flooded my mind. I knew God had spoken. But I had no idea how it was about to change my life.

Looking back, I now see that this is where my journey to **catholicity** began. Though I had been quietly meditating on the unity of the church for most of my life, on that Sunday morning God got my attention. He confronted me with the question that has stirred my passion and my prayers for the church ever since: If there is "one body and … one Lord" (Ephesians 4:4–5), what does this really mean?

MY JOURNEY TO CHRISTIAN FAITH

I was born into a Christian home in which my parents deeply loved God, the Scriptures, and the church we faithfully attended several times a week. I cannot recall a time when I did *not* care about spiritual realities or the things of God. Aside from a brief period of wrestling with doubts in college, I have loved God and desired to know him my entire life.

I have often pondered the words of Jesus and Peter in John 6:67–69. Here we discover that many who "believed" in Jesus eventually abandoned him. Jesus even asked the disciples at one point if they, too, wanted to leave. "You do not want to leave too, do you?" Jesus asked his disciples. Simon Peter answered, "Lord, to whom shall we go? You have the words of eternal life. We have come to believe and to know that you are the Holy One of God."

Perhaps you can identify with this conversation. Peter says that he and the other disciples "have come to believe and to know." The perfect tense in the Greek literally renders the phrase as "We have entered a state of belief and knowledge that has continued until the present time." When we come to "know" Jesus, we enter a state of belief and knowledge that will continue. As I look back on my life, I have come to see that the question of *when* or *how* I "entered" the faith is not the most important question to answer. Not everyone will have a good answer to this question or be able to pinpoint one particular moment. The real question you must always face is quite simple: Do you really *know* Jesus?

After sixty-one years, I have found that no one satisfies or explains me like Jesus does. Don't get me wrong. I read widely and learn from many great thinkers, even many non-Christians. But Jesus' words alone have eternal life. They reside inside me as the *living* truth.

THREE LIFE-CHANGING CONVERSIONS

Several years ago, a friend told me I had experienced three great spiritual conversions. Though he wasn't entirely accurate, I still found his observation useful. My first conversion was when I came to consciously follow Jesus as a boy in February 1956, just weeks before I turned seven. I was not completely converted from a life of sin and rebellion, since I was still a small boy. But my church background was one in which "personal conversion," with its attendant prayer of commitment, was *how* you came to know Jesus. Being such a young child, I had a load of questions and really wanted answers. One evening, I knew I needed to make sure that I really loved Jesus. I bowed in prayer with my mother and asked Jesus to save me. I would experience many times when this conversion model of faith led me to doubt if I had "done it right." In time, I realized that what I did and exactly how I did it were not the real issues. Again the question I had to answer was: Do you know Jesus and do you love him *now*? Or to use the words of the gospel of John, Was I in a state of faith and the knowledge of Jesus that is eternal life?

My second conversion came during my college years and the four years following graduation. I met many different Christians with diverse beliefs. After graduating from college, I was a church planter for four years while I completed graduate studies. Some of my theology was quite unsettled. I had encountered a strong view of God's sovereignty (often called Calvinism) under the tutelage of one of my professors. I heard the opposite view from another professor I dearly loved. Three times a week, for a whole semester, I heard the first professor teach about God's power and providence. But when this class ended, I was still unconvinced, believing that human freedom was being denied.

Over the years, I continued to question my understanding of God's nature and providence. Then, on New Year's Day 1977, I found a quiet place and poured out my heart to God. I happily embraced the insights of some of the church's greatest theologians regarding divine sovereignty and human responsibility. Strange as it might seem to some, I felt a freedom I had never known.

It would be an understatement to say that my life and ministry were powerfully changed. I began to preach what I saw in the Scriptures, but this did not sit well with my not very "doctrinally defined" congregation. I am sure now I could have handled much of this transformation better if I had been a bit wiser. I am equally sure some would have resisted the message of divine sovereignty, no matter how winsomely I presented it. Embracing human freedom and divine sovereignty is often done badly. Far too much harmful argumentation surrounds this subject. People in the modern American church do not respond easily to the idea of God reigning over all things.

In my forties, I became deeply immersed in the question behind this book: What is the church? I sincerely wanted to understand John 17 and Ephesians 4. I confess I held a rather simplistic view of the church. For me, this meant I believed the church was primarily an *invisible* reality that consisted of those born of God's Spirit. I secretly doubted this exclusively "invisible" church concept. It appeared to fall short of the New Testament description of a vibrant and visible community. But out of fear of ridicule and misunderstanding, I rarely discussed these questions with peers.

Then, in 1995, everything changed for me. As I was saying the Apostles' Creed during a Sunday morning worship service I experienced my third conversion. The Holy Spirit took my heart to the "Lord's Prayer" recorded in the gospel of John:

> My prayer is not for them alone. I pray also for those who will believe in me through their message, that all of them may be one, Father, just as you are in me and I am in you. May they also be in us so that the world may believe that you have sent me. I have given them the glory that you gave me, that they may be one as we are one—I in them and you in me—so that they may be brought to complete unity. Then the world will know that you sent me and have loved them even as you have loved me.
>
> *John 17:20–23*

For me there was a special irony in being brought to these words. I had preached the Scriptures, mostly verse by verse, for twenty-one years. I had completed a sixteen-year pastorate in May 1992. For the last two years of that pastorate, I had preached through the gospel of John. My last sermon text at the end of those years was John 17:20–23.

HOW GOD DIRECTED ME

As I soaked my soul in the prayer of Jesus (John 17), my vision for the unity of the church increased. My love for the church became more than love for a concept; instead, it developed into a deep, growing love for the church as God's people.

As I unpacked the insights the Holy Spirit was giving to me, I sensed two things. First, I realized that I couldn't love what I didn't know. I knew very little about the *whole* Christian church, even though I had a good grasp of church history. I knew there were three different historic Christian churches—Catholic, Protestant, and Orthodox. But I knew very little about what these three great churches believed and why. I knew something about the intra-Protestant differences via disagreements and schisms. But I knew much less about the core truths shared by all Christians everywhere. I soon discovered what is called **classical Christianity.** I read materials from various churches, traditions, and theologians. I tried to read what churches had written about themselves rather than what others had written against them. What my reading and listening uncovered was nothing short of amazing. It became clear that there was much to learn from the wider body of the Christian church.

Second, I knew that I couldn't be satisfied with loving a *concept* of the church. So I set out to find God's people, to get to know people outside of my own tradition. At first, this seemed like a daunting task, but I began by taking one small step at a time. I made it a personal priority to meet with Christians who were different from me. Before long, I was relating to an ever-widening circle of new friends.

THE JOURNEY TO OTHERS

I would often ask God to lead me to different Christians, just as I had asked him to lead me to non-Christians with whom I could share the gospel. On an airplane, I once encountered a young priest across the aisle reading a book by a twentieth-century **Roman Catholic** theologian I had discovered, Hans Urs von Balthasar (1905–1988). A conversation ensued, and a friendship was born.

Another time, while speaking at a seminary, I met a group of Catholic monks. They invited me to visit their monastery, and as a result of that visit, my life was powerfully changed. Out of these relationships and the peace and quiet of places like that monastery, fresh wind came into my soul. What united all of us, despite our differences, was the one Christ we knew and loved as brothers and sisters. I had no category for this kind of love and the way it brought an immediate sense of unity to our relationships.

During this time, a man from a local Nazarene church asked me to participate in a dialogue with a Roman Catholic theologian. Nervously, I said yes, knowing in my spirit that this event could mark my life. That evening was electric. The moderator was a local Chicago television news anchor. The place was packed. I knew what questions we would discuss, but I had never met this priest. My fear was that he would destroy my arguments and that I would let down my side. My old fears of ridicule were alive and well. They proved groundless. We had an honest dialogue and agreed on some things and clearly disagreed on others. But my presence there still felt like betrayal. I came to realize the emotions inside my heart were driven by fear.

I decided to analyze my fears and came to see that fear—brought about by real or perceived dangers—was negatively impacting much of my spiritual life and bringing with it deep anxiety. Earlier, I would have harbored doubts that some of my new friends were real Christians. It began to feel as though I was betraying my calling and growing soft in my doctrinal convictions. Some people, even close friends, were suggesting as much. The Internet was a double-edged sword for me. It provided a great forum to write about the church, but it also became a place for criticism, as some began to suggest I had taken a wrong turn and fallen into doctrinal error.

During the late 1990s, at a church renewal conference in Dubuque, Iowa, I began to experience a deepening love for God's people. This event included Methodists, Lutherans, Presbyterians, Disciples of Christ (the Christian Church), Roman Catholics, American Baptists, Episcopalians, and Congregationalists (United Church of Christ). I had always distrusted many of the people from these groups since they represented the more liberal (mainline) denominations. Now here I was, meeting and praying with them.

The mission I had founded, ACT 3, sponsored this event.[1] The conference featured five plenary speakers—Donald Bloesch, J. I. Packer, William Abraham, Carl Braaten, and myself—all of whom were from very different church communions. Workshops were led by both Protestants and Roman Catholics. While at the conference, I also had my first encounter with an Orthodox Christian. The editor of *Touchstone* magazine, James Kushiner, and I began a warm conversation that has led to a lasting friendship.

A PROPHECY

Driving back to Illinois, a close friend said to me, "Just as we now crossed the Mississippi River, John, so you have crossed a river in your own life. You can never go back to where you were or who you were before this week." Looking back, his words now sound prophetic. Indeed, I had crossed a river, and there was no going back. My passion for unity was driving me forward and would soon define my entire life. I didn't have a name for what I was thinking back then, but I now call it **missional-ecumenism**. In the pages ahead, I will unpack more of what this term means.

Sadly, I would soon discover that some Christian friends were not interested in sharing my joy. Some of their negative responses prompted me to write articles and letters to explain what I was discovering—material that became the seed that finally flowered into this book.

Today, my passion for the church has led me to monasteries and Methodists, to Anglicans and the Assemblies of God, and to a growing respect for Mennonites and Moravians. It took me, an evangelical and a Reformed Protestant, deeper into the words of Luther and Calvin, who left a profound mark on a large portion of the Christian church. To my great surprise, it propelled me back to the church fathers and the Christian past—a past that is both Roman Catholic and Orthodox. In Catholicism, I discovered a community so vast that it overwhelmed me in its richness, beauty, and diversity. Over time, I came to love this community, a community I had once feared so deeply. In Orthodoxy, I found an entirely different community—one that seemed so strange to me at first, with its icons and long liturgies. But my journey into friendship with Orthodox brothers and sisters would prove more beneficial than I could ever have imagined.

A NEW DECADE AND A NEW OUTLOOK

Over the last fifteen years, I have meditated faithfully on the words of John 17. I now regularly recite the Apostles' Creed. I have taken up the ancient church practice of daily spiritual reading (*lectio divina*) and have read the church fathers regularly. One day, as I was reflecting on these things, I realized that the idea of the church that I had embraced for well over forty years was just too small. God had taken me on a journey and had deepened my love for his church in ways I could have never expected or imagined.

Your experience may be different from mine. But wherever you are in your understanding of the church, I believe God wants to tear down walls that keep you from other Christians. A small view of the church limits our ability to love as God loves and affects our ongoing witness to the watching world. I pray that God will use my story to inspire you to undertake your own journey toward catholicity so you will embrace a richer and fuller understanding of the church of Jesus Christ.

QUESTIONS FOR DISCUSSION AND REFLECTION

1. What "conversions" have you experienced in your life that have profoundly shaped your own story?

2. How do you "know" you have passed from death to life and are in union with the living Christ?

3. If you were asked to tell your own story about your faith and your church experience, how would you describe it at this point in your life?

chapter three

Searching for the Elusive Truth

This unfortunate idea—that the basis of spiritual unity must stand in uniformity of doctrine—has been the poisoned spring of all the dissensions that have torn Christ's body.

John Watson

Do not call yourselves Lutherans, call yourselves Christians. Has Luther been crucified for the world?

Martin Luther

BEGINNING AROUND THE MIDDLE of the first century, the nascent church found itself mired in disunity. Paul's Corinthian letters bear ample witness to this reality: "I appeal to you, brothers and sisters, in the name of our Lord Jesus Christ, that all of you agree with one another in what you say and that there be no divisions among you, but that you be perfectly united in mind and thought" (1 Corinthians 1:10).

What is strikingly clear is the way Paul categorized this problem when he wrote about the ministry of the Holy Spirit. In a passage dealing with life in the Spirit and what it actually looks like, he concluded, "The acts of the sinful nature are obvious: sexual immorality, impurity and debauchery; idolatry and witchcraft; hatred, *discord*, jealousy, fits of rage, selfish ambition, *dissensions*, *factions* and envy; drunkenness, orgies and the like. I warn you, as I did before, that those who live like this will not inherit the kingdom of God" (Galatians 5:19 – 21, italics added).

Note the italicized words: *discord*, *dissensions*, and *factions*. When James tells us that "fights and quarrels" among Christians come from "desires that battle within you" (James 4:1 – 2), it becomes patently clear that disunity was a very real problem, even for the earliest Christians.

THE NEW TESTAMENT PORTRAIT

Participation in the life of the church was never an optional part of following Jesus. Every Christian's life in the apostolic era was deeply rooted in the corporate life of the church. The New Testament paints the picture of a generous and large-spirited group of people who understood that the basis for their unity was their oneness with the risen Christ. Their life as a community was dynamic and expansive. It was founded on an experience of unity that was anchored in the Trinity—the eternal, interpersonal communion of God—and thus the New Testament sees unity as a reality to be protected.

During the apostolic era, Peter and Paul openly quarreled about the extent to which the precepts of the Jewish law should apply to Gentile converts. A generation later, the Johannine communities in Asia Minor argued over whether the interior anointing of the Holy Spirit was a sufficient control for Christian ethics. And this was just the beginning of doctrinal disagreements within the church.

Despite these disagreements on points of doctrine, the New Testament, as well as the subsequent postapostolic record, reveals that there was still a deep commitment among the leaders to preserve the church as one family. In the New Testament, we find an ongoing tension between the unity of their common experience of Christ and their disagreements over points of doctrine. These leaders wisely recognized that while Christ should be at the center as Lord of the church, every effort must be made to preserve unity. I believe we, too, must live within the dynamism of these two commitments—a dynamism that comes from the Holy Spirit, not our brilliance or energy.

DIVISION BECAME THE NORM

By the tenth century, the church took on the appearance of a federation. In the West, the form paralleled Roman patterns of hierarchy; in the East, there was a less rigid but plainly patriarchal expression. By the medieval period, the visible church was tragically split into two huge and virtually unrelated branches—East and West (1054). Then, the papacy, considered to be the center of unity in the West, was moved to Avignon. Eventually, disagreements and political disputes began to overwhelm the fragile unity of the West. The Protestant Reformation led to a split in the Western church in the sixteenth century, and the religious wars that followed were bloody and destructive.

With a history of division and disunity, it is no wonder that most contemporary American churches have a vague understanding of unity. Most Christians today have settled for a "small" view of the church—a church divided and fractured. Sadly, each of these subdivisions has also been exported beyond America to the global church. Our spirit of divisiveness has spread like a pandemic. Even our best and brightest leaders tenaciously defend the "small" church mind-set.

My thesis is simple: This "small" view of the church harms the mission of Christ. It spreads the seeds of **sectarianism** and forces us to choose our friends and enemies based on whether or not we are in complete agreement with one another on specific matters of doctrine. Sectarianism has kept Christians from working toward visible expressions of unity in the twenty-first century.

HOW A DEEPLY CONSERVATIVE CHRISTIAN DISCOVERED THE CHURCH

In 1992, I became the full-time president of a teaching mission that came into existence to reform and renew the church. This mission began to embrace a deeper vision of the church when speaking and teaching about church unity became a major aspect of my calling.[1]

I was born into a very conservative home and church in the American South. I still recall the first stirrings of the Civil Rights era. As I attended my all-white church during my childhood, I do not recall hearing discussions about the unity of the church or the struggle for justice and civil rights. I knew there were many different kinds of churches, even in my small town of less than ten thousand people. (The Catholic church was the smallest church, and all the churches were segregated.)

After six years in a military prep school I enrolled at the University of Alabama. It was 1967, and integration had just begun to impact the South. My college church was an all-white Baptist congregation. At the time, I thought to myself, "I'm going to find a church in Tuscaloosa that is biblical." But deep inside, I had some nagging doubts about what made for a *biblical* church. My certainty that I could find the perfect biblical church was wavering. I wasn't sure how I felt about my denomination's practice of excluding other Christians from the Lord's Supper. In fact, by the second term of my freshman year, I had begun to question many things about my church.

At this point I came in contact with Campus Crusade for Christ. My life and faith were profoundly altered as I learned to personally share my faith in Christ. As I think back on those days, I believe I was more affected by doing mission with other Christians than by the witnessing experience itself. Through Campus Crusade, I experienced other expressions of the church for the first time, including a house church in which we celebrated the Lord's Supper in a circle. (I thought this surely had to be a New Testament way of doing it!)

Since college, I have celebrated the Eucharist in both cathedral-like buildings and small house churches. More important, I have come to see how crucial the Eucharist is for *all* Christians. The key truth is to be found in the presence of Jesus Christ with his people, not in the fighting over the outward forms a group has adopted for serving the sacrament.[2]

MOVING TO THE CENTER OF AMERICAN EVANGELICALISM

My growing love for Christ's mission led me to transfer to Wheaton College in 1969. Its motto is: "For Christ and His Kingdom." I earned two degrees during my time at Wheaton and now have the privilege of teaching there as an adjunct professor of evangelism. I loved its evangelical impulse and embraced the mission of the college.

But by far the greatest thing that happened to me while a student was my growing encounter with Christ through the church. I met faculty and students who came from diverse backgrounds, ethnicities, cultures, and denominations. My teachers agreed on basic doctrinal issues but participated in a broad dialogue about many things Christians did not agree about. For the first time, I began to think for myself. I was invited to raise questions. I remember arguing with a Lutheran student until late in the night and fiercely debating several Calvinists who were too fatalistic for my tastes. I lost some theological baggage, visited different types of churches, and, above all, kept reading and asking questions. Still, despite these positive experiences, in practice I retained a rather narrow view of the church. It would still be several years before my questions would lead to life-changing answers.

A PASTOR WHO SEARCHED

After college and graduate school, I entered the pastorate, first as a suburban church planter and then for sixteen years in a congregation in Wheaton. During my twenty years of pastoral ministry, I met a lot of other ministers, including clergy from mainline Protestant churches, with more theologically progressive stances. During those early years in ministry, I even met a few Roman Catholic priests and got to know them as friends. (Most of the ordinary lay Catholics I met in those days sought my help in their search for personal faith in Christ.)

I still recall the first time my wife and I invited a local Catholic priest to dinner. It was the second year in my first pastorate. I was amazed at how many misconceptions I had embraced about Catholicism. I was even more amazed when I was asked to speak at a community Thanksgiving service at a Catholic church. These were the 1970s, the early days of post-Vatican II Catholicism. Rapid changes were taking place—changes I did not fully understand at the time. My staunchest evangelical friends insisted that Vatican II changed nothing. Only later would I learn how profoundly wrong they were.

Some of these evangelical friends insisted that Roman Catholics were members of a false church. (Of course, we evangelicals believed we were in the right church.) Sadly, this attempt to determine who is in a false church continues to this day. Some Catholics and Protestants still treat one another with much suspicion. The bigger problem was that even evangelical Protestants didn't agree with one another. (What is commonly agreed on as the definition of an **evangelical** is a slim list of ideas and doctrines.) In truth, we disagreed about many important doctrines: our view of the inspiration of Scripture; how we define faith, baptism, and the Lord's Supper; church order; the doctrine of the future; the gifts of the Holy Spirit; the doctrine of the human will; and the nature of how God's grace works in salvation. The more I studied these internal evangelical debates, the longer the list grew. Something was wrong with this approach, but I still couldn't see exactly what it was.

As the charismatic movement exploded, I wondered, "How can this be? These are not mainstream evangelicals." But then I experienced the fresh wind of God personally. Silently, I kept searching. Something seemed wrong with my narrow understanding of church, but I didn't know what to do with my questions and fears. Eventually, I discovered a wonderful liberty in letting go of the need to always be right!

But what gave me the greatest anxiety was not my attempt to figure it all out; the biggest problem was the personal ramifications I'd experience by acknowledging that I fellowshipped with Christians in different Christian churches. Friendships would be challenged, and people would question my faith. For as long as I could, I tried to play it safe, denying what I was seeing and experiencing.

But trips overseas further influenced my life. I saw the church in a whole new light when I went to India and Latin America and encountered contexts so unlike my own. India was the first major blow to my "small" church view. Latin America shook me even more profoundly, especially with its mixture of believing and unbelieving Catholicism practiced in ways that are sometimes foreign to orthodox Christian beliefs.

My small view of God's church was crumbling by the early 1990s when I had begun reciting the Apostles' Creed. In the midst of this season, the Holy Spirit moved powerfully in my heart to remove much blindness and fear. I began to humble myself before some basic biblical commands:

- "This is his command: to believe in the name of his Son, Jesus Christ, and to love one another as he commanded us" (1 John 3:23).
- "Dear friends, since God so loved us, we also ought to love one another. No one has ever seen God; but if we love one another, God lives in us and his love is made complete in us" (1 John 4:11–12).
- "We love because he first loved us. If we say we love God yet hate a brother or sister, we are liars. For if we do not love a fellow believer, whom we have seen, we cannot love God, whom we have not seen. And he has given us this command: Those who love God must also love one another" (1 John 4:19–21).

God was using his Word and the witness of his people to profoundly enlarge my view of the church. A passion for unity would eventually lead me to reconsider the prayer of Jesus in John 17 and radically change my understanding of biblical oneness.

QUESTIONS FOR DISCUSSION AND REFLECTION

1. What kind of picture do you have of the New Testament church? Did unity really matter to the leaders of the early church? Why or why not?

2. Why do you think division has become the norm in the Christian church? What practical actions can we take now in the context of being so obviously divided?

3. How does your love for Christ relate to your love for his church? Try to be specific about the ways in which these two are related for you.

chapter four

The Jesus Prayer for Our Unity

Although the church of Jesus Christ is found in many different places, she is one church, not many. After all, there are many rays of sunlight, but only one sun. A tree has many boughs, each slightly different from others, but all drawing their strength from one source. Many streams may flow down a hillside, but they all originate from the same spring. In exactly the same way each local congregation belongs to the one true church.

Cyprian

JESUS' PRAYER IN JOHN 17 is very specific. The Son asks the Father to glorify him in his impending death and resurrection. He prays for his immediate disciples, who will soon be formally commissioned to carry on his work. I find his words deeply moving.

> My prayer is not for them alone. I pray also for those who will believe in me through their message, that all of them may be one, Father, just as you are in me and I am in you. May they also be in us so that the world may believe that you have sent me. I have given them the glory that you gave me, that they may be one as we are one—I in them and you in me—so that they may be brought to complete unity. Then the world will know that you sent me and have loved them even as you have loved me.
>
> *John 17:20–23*

This entire prayer in John 17, if taken in a literal sense, should really be called "the Lord's Prayer." It is a prayer that only our Lord could offer to the Father, not one we can pray as he did. It is also the longest and most comprehensive recorded prayer of Jesus. But note carefully that Jesus doesn't pray just for his immediate disciples. He prays for the entire church—for all of those who will believe in him throughout the ages to follow. He prays that all believers "may be one as we [Father and Son] are one."

A TEXT BADLY INTERPRETED

I can think of few other passages of Holy Scripture (at least passages so important for the well-being of the church) for which there have been so many wrong explanations. Some teachers seem to major on what this text does *not* mean. Many of their interpretations appear to be reactions to what they believe are mistaken ideas. Consider a few I have heard through the years:

- We should never try to unite different churches or congregations. The union of churches or denominations is not in view here. Jesus is not interested in such unity.
- We should never engage in serious dialogue with churches that we believe to be unfaithful to the truth. We will become disobedient if we follow this course.
- There is no common mission that churches are called to engage in; thus there is no reason to work together to achieve Christ's mission in our communities.
- There is no concern in this prayer for the worldwide church, at least as seen in a *visible* form, since this will lead to ecumenism, a great twentieth-century enemy of the gospel.
- We must always keep in the forefront of our practice the serious biblical warnings about compromise and false teaching (see Deuteronomy 7:1–6; 2 Corinthians 6:14; Revelation 18:4). These great truths always trump concern for visible unity among churches and Christians.

Such fears and concerns often cause commentators to read the idea of *invisible* unity into their interpretation of John 17. They argue that the invisible church, consisting of all true Christians, cannot be divided, so it must be the invisible unity of the church that Jesus is praying for here. This point, it seems to me, is partially true. But to assume that the invisible church is the "one holy catholic and apostolic church" of the Nicene Creed or that it is the answer to this prayer is a serious interpretive mistake. If Jesus is praying for a oneness we already possess, then this prayer has nothing to do with what we should be doing right now. Just ask yourself a simple question: Why would Jesus pray for something that is already true? Why does he pray for us to be brought to complete unity if it is something that we *already* possess?

While it is true that all who believe in Christ are one in him, it is not true that what he prays for here has already come to pass. We all know that the unity Jesus prays for is far from a reality in the church. It's not evident in most of our local congregations. A breakdown of church unity is the most commonly cited problem in almost every congregational study of the church undertaken since the 1980s.

RELATIONAL UNITY

So what *is* Jesus praying for? Our *relational unity*, I suggest. He is praying for a unity between persons that is rooted in their relationships with one another. In a profound sense, the unity Jesus prays for here is also *spiritual*—a unity that cannot be created or sustained by us. To be clear, I am not using *spiritual* as a synonym for *invisible*. Confusing spiritual unity with invisible unity is the major flaw in all the arguments that use this term to explain away the relational intention of John 17.

We will consider a much better way to understand spiritual unity in chapter 6, a way that is both spiritual and visible. For now, it is important to note that if the unity Jesus prays for is between people in relationships, then this unity can be lost to divisions, rivalries, factions, and church splits. Relational unity—even though it is spiritual—can be quenched and grieved through the breaking of relationships in the body of Christ.

We should also be clear that Jesus is not addressing the issue of denominations (since they did not exist), nor is he talking about universal church councils (which also did not exist). Most biblical scholars, including many modern Catholic scholars, agree with these points.

Jesus' prayer for relational unity simply means he is praying that all his followers will live as he lived. In particular, his prayer points to his personal relationship with the Father. Christians believe that the second person of the Trinity, the **Logos**, was incarnated in the man Jesus. Jesus lived fully and completely as a human person, and in his humanity, he lived each day in total dependence on his Father. This relationship, lived by the fullness of the Holy Spirit, was one of perfect unity. It is this relational aspect that is clearly in view in John 17.

It becomes especially clear that relational unity is the goal when Jesus prays in verse 23 that his disciples will be *"brought to complete unity"* (italics added). Consider your own relationship with Jesus. Each of us already has spiritual unity in our relationship with Jesus through the work of the Holy Spirit, but we do not experience this unity in a relational sense unless we are "brought" into it through a day-to-day interaction with Jesus.

Spiritual unity, while real and true, must be experienced relationally, which opens up a dynamic, ongoing movement toward unity—in our lives as individuals and in our relationships with one another—as we share in the divine life of the Trinity. When Christians live out their spiritual unity with Jesus in the way that he prayed for, the results will be exactly what Jesus asked the Father to give us: "Then the world will know that you [the Father] sent me and have loved them even as you have loved me" (verse 23). The church will be a visible example of the relational and spiritual unity of the triune God.

DIVIDE AND MULTIPLY

Theologian Ben Witherington has rightly noted that the first law of American Protestant ecclesiology seems to be "Thou shalt divide and multiply." I learned this principle while serving in my first pastorate. My denomination desperately wanted to plant new churches. The local church I served had originally split from another church, which itself had been part of a third church where I had previously been a member. Confused? To put it simply, here were three congregations, all within five miles of each other in two suburban cities, and in each case a new church had formed from a split due to quarreling, petty personal disputes, and jealousy. Sadly, though we were part of the same denomination, we were encouraged to separate for the sake of mission.

One day I decided to ask a denominational executive why they encouraged church splits. He eagerly informed me that dividing churches was actually a healthy way to reach new people for Christ! I expressed my concern about schism and the obvious lack of holiness I saw in these three churches. Later I would hear this man tell other ministers that dividing churches, through any means, would multiply churches. We were all told this was a good goal. To put it mildly, I was appalled. I couldn't imagine how encouraging schism could ever be right. But then again, this is America!

Unfortunately, a passion for truth and unity are rarely found in the same church, let alone a denomination. Ben Witherington states:

> There is always a tension in the church between unity among believers and truth as it is understood and held by believers. Protestantism has tended to hold up Truth, with a capital *T*, while intoning unity with a lowercase *u*, with the end result that Protestant churches and denominations have proved endlessly divisive and factious. On the other hand, Catholicism and Orthodoxy have held up Unity with a capital *U*, and at least from a Protestant viewpoint this has been at the expense of Truth. In others words, no part of the church has adequately gotten the balance between truth and unity right, it would seem.[1]

Deep inside, I had known for many years that the stance I took for capital *T* truth over and against capital *U* unity was a false dichotomy. Why couldn't we choose to embrace both Truth and Unity? Did we always have to choose one over the other? Where was the common ground that would bring us together?

WHY DOES THIS MATTER?

In John 17, Jesus says that his mission literally hangs on the answer to this prayer. The mission of Jesus seems to be so closely linked with the relational unity of the church that the world will not fully understand and experience God's love until we are "brought" into the experience of this unity. Given what we have seen throughout the history of the church, I have to wonder, "How has the church survived as a witness to God's love in the world, given our egregious schisms, constant faithlessness, and corruption?"

Historian Clyde Manschreck suggests that the message of the early Christian church has been "abused, institutionalized, abandoned, [and] rationalized."[2] But we can't escape the fact the church is still here, sometimes in poor health but occasionally pulsating with power and great blessing, as we see in the modern-day house churches of China. Yet more often than not, the church is "lukewarm," alive and breathing but distracted from her true purpose and in obvious need of divine chastisement (Revelation 3:16).

I urge every church to regularly ask, "What does Christ *really* think of our church?" An honest assessment might be troubling, but asking the question can lead to repentance and a recognition that the identity of the church is not bound up in our own sense of self-importance.

The New Testament church began with the foundation of Peter's confession of faith — the divine revelation that Jesus was the Messiah (Matthew 16:13 – 18). Following Jesus' death and resurrection, the power of the Holy Spirit was poured out on the earliest disciples (Acts 2), and the festival of Pentecost became a birthday celebration for God's people as an empowered group of disciples emerged. These disciples did not bear the sword or engage in the politics of the day; they simply brought with them a message of God's love for all people, expressed by caring for those in need and serving one another whenever possible. Congregations grew, even in the face of intense opposition. Not even the powers of hell could stop the mission of the church.

Since that day, the church has marched like a mighty army across the globe. From the martyrdom of Stephen (Act 7) through massive waves of slaughter brought about by Roman persecution and through Muslim hordes attacking Christian lands and twentieth-century Communist opposition, the church — despite its problems and flaws — continues to grow. Today, most of this growth is happening not in the Western world but in the churches of China, India, Africa, and Latin America. It seems fair to say that the church cannot be stopped. Why? Because it is *God's* church. Though there have been times when it seemed as if the light carried by the church of Jesus Christ would be extinguished, God has kept his promise to his people. His church continues to grow, even where he has administered corrective discipline (cf. Revelation 2–3).

But what has kept the church going in the midst of all this suffering and trial? I believe the story of history demonstrates that the church stayed faithful, not by means of a vague belief in the concept of God, but through a living and active faith in the God who is love (1 John 4:8, 16). Scripture teaches us that the very substance and nature of God is love. All divine activity flows from the heart of a loving God.

This "new religion" of love was not "an external system of ritual sacrifice ... but an internal flooding of the mind and spirit with divine love and understanding."[3] The power of God's Spirit transformed the first believers, resulting in lives characterized by joy and peace. In addition, the early church "understood itself for what it was intended to be: *a spiritual kingdom sharing spiritual truth with a troubled world.*"[4]

GOD'S LOVE IN ACTION

Jesus' prayer for unity, understood in the right way, is really a prayer about God's love in action. Jesus prayed, "Then the world will know that you sent me and have *loved them even as you have loved me*" (John 17:23, italics added). The theme of God's love for the world is so common in John's writings that I see it as the special emphasis of the apostle in both the fourth gospel and his letters.

Are we so comfortable with the idea that God loves us (John 3:16) that this great mystery no longer moves us? Have we been so conditioned to think of God's love for us as individuals that we fail to consider what this means for a congregation? For a city? Or for the worldwide church of God?

The New Testament churches were made up of people from diverse backgrounds. Christianity was a religion with a universal scope and a global vision. It was a faith that welcomed everyone—regardless of social status, ethnicity, gender, or wealth—into a family in which relationships were founded on a common Savior and unity was formed out of diversity.

> So in Christ Jesus you are all children of God through faith, for all of you who were baptized into Christ have clothed your-selves with Christ. There is neither Jew nor Gentile, neither slave nor free, neither male nor female, for you are all one in Christ Jesus.
>
> *Galatians 3:26–28*

Unity in Christ—rooted in the triune love of Father, Son, and Holy Spirit—is clearly a major theme of the New Testament writings. The biblical doctrine of our inclusion in Christ created both a new ethic (a way of living) and a new community (the basis for human relationships). Paul, in his letters to the churches, taught that ethnicity, gender, and social status no longer were determinative factors for relating to God or others in the family of God. Everyone in the church is "one in Christ Jesus." This is the spiritual and relational reality that comes about when the divinely infused love of Christ is poured out into the hearts of all who believe.

John taught the early church that this unity in Christ is the reason why "we love" both God and others (1 John 4:19–21). Peter wrote that "above all" we should "love each other deeply" (1 Peter 4:8). Early believers were urged to "make every effort to keep the unity of the Spirit through the bond of peace" (Ephesians 4:3). Love for one another was the whole point of the new life in Christ.

But the church began to experience the loss of this shared love, even before the first century drew to a close. In the last book of the New Testament, we read Jesus' words to the churches and find that things had already begun to drift from his purpose.

> "To the angel of the church in Ephesus write:
> These are the words of him who holds the seven stars in his right hand and walks among the seven golden lamp-stands. I know your deeds, your hard work and your perse-verance. I know that you cannot tolerate wicked people, that you have tested those who claim to be apostles but are not, and have found them false. You have persevered and have endured hardships for my name, and have not grown weary.

> Yet I hold this against you: You have forsaken the love you had at first. Consider how far you have fallen! Repent and do the things you did at first. If you do not repent, I will come to you and remove your lampstand from its place."
>
> *Revelation 2:1–5*

Here is a church praised for keeping faith. These Christians worked hard, persevered in their faith, and dealt with false teachers. They had not grown weary as they endured hardships and suffering. But they lacked something vital that would eventually lead to the death of their congregation; they lacked love. The church of Ephesus is a reminder that we can have sound doctrine and a great ministry, but if we lack love and are marked by divisions and quarrels, the consequences are severe. Right doctrine and good deeds are no guarantee that a church truly loves others.

Jesus' prayer for unity teaches us that even when we disagree on matters of doctrine or practice, we should avoid building barriers between ourselves and other Christians. We must be willing to accept those who are accepted by God and belong to him. May our prayer reflect the will of Jesus, as we pray that our love will prevail by the power of the Spirit—for the unity of God's church.

QUESTIONS FOR DISCUSSION AND REFLECTION

1. Why do you think we come up with so many explanations for John 17:20–23 that refuse to take seriously what our Lord actually prayed for?

2. How would you explain the idea of *relational unity*? How could it impact your family and friendships?

3. Why do you believe we set Truth and Unity against each other as opposites? What can we do to stop doing this?

4. What would Christ say to your church about its commitment to him and to unity with other churches?

chapter five

Our Greatest Apologetic

I believe very strongly in the principle and practice of the purity of the visible church, but I have seen churches that have fought for purity and are merely hotbeds of ugliness. No longer is there any observable, loving, personal relationship even in their own midst, let alone with other true Christians.

Francis A. Schaeffer

I TEACH APOLOGETICS. Apologetics has to do with the defense of the Christian faith against anti-Christian ideas. Francis Schaeffer, the late evangelical apologist, once said the greatest apologetic for evangelism was *the oneness of Christians*. He believed our truest identifying mark was love.

Schaeffer wrote, "Love—and the unity it attests to—is *the mark* Christ gave Christians to wear before the world" (italics added).[1] I believe Schaeffer was exactly right. His statement accurately reflects what Jesus taught in John 13–17 and what the apostle John stressed in his writings:

- "A new command I give you: Love one another. As I have loved you, so you must love one another. By this everyone will know that you are my disciples, if you love one another" (John 13:34–35).
- "And this is his command: to believe in the name of his son, Jesus Christ, and to love one another as he commanded us" (1 John 3:23).

- "Dear friends, let us love one another, for love comes from God. Everyone who loves has been born of God and knows God. Whoever does not love does not know God, because God is love" (1 John 4:7–8).

Friedrich Nietzsche (1844–1900), the anti-Christian philosopher, once said the problem with the church is that it is "human, all too human." I believe Nietzsche was right. But this "human" church is still Christ's body. Complacent Christians need to be regularly reminded that they have been brought into the church by God's grace to become more and more like Christ.

As an apologist, Francis Schaeffer also recognized that the church exists not simply for itself but for the sake of a watching world. How we act and treat one another really matters, because our actions represent the nature and identity of God to those who do not know him. Schaeffer states, "Anything that an individual Christian or Christian group does that fails to show the simultaneous balance of the holiness of God and the love of God presents to a watching world not a demonstration of the God who exists but a caricature of the God who exists."[2]

We have given the world an ugly caricature of God, and multitudes cannot hear our good news. They hear us opposing their politics with strident moral pronouncements. They know that we oppose their lifestyle and feel condemned. A plethora of recent studies has revealed this sad fact and provides another reason for my belief that a "small" church mind-set directly hinders Christ's mission.[3]

BACK TO THE FUTURE

As noted in chapter 1, the way forward for the church lies in the past—in a return to the prayer of Jesus and core orthodoxy. We must have a starting point that will allow us to be clear about what really matters and why it matters. We must know who we are, as the people of God, and how to speak about Christ faithfully. When we have clarity on the essentials, we are free to confidently move forward into a deeper understanding of the church, one that can be lived out in our congregations without fear or the need to condemn or avoid others. Without this common ground of doctrinal orthodoxy, our unity is merely experiential, and we are prone to drift from the truth of Christian faith.

On the night before he was killed, Jesus looked beyond his little band of disciples and embraced you and me when he prayed for those who would believe in him nearly twenty centuries later. The Spirit used the sending of the first disciples in the same way that he used the Father's sending of the Son into the world (John 17:18). When we come to the end of John 17, we encounter the last of three concentric circles. In the final circle, while Jesus refers to heavenly realities (verse 24), his primary concern remains the unity of his people on earth. In fact, twice he prays that we will be one, just as he and the Father are one, so that we will "be brought to complete unity" (verse 23).

The real indicator of the church's faithfulness is not successful evangelization; it is our oneness. Cults and false religions can prosper and grow numerically—Islam grows at a remarkable pace, for instance. Other religions reach people and make converts, sometimes better than the Christian church does. In fact, the fastest-growing religious category in America over the last decade is made up of those who describe themselves as having "no religion." Anyone can grow—but unity is much harder to manufacture.

THE PATTERN FOR OUR UNITY

The Father, Son, and Holy Spirit are one in essence (being). According to John 17, the goal of our unity is the same as that of the triune God: to reveal God's love to the world (verse 21). With this in mind, Jesus' prayer raises an important question for us: In what sense can our unity as Christians be compared to the unity we see in the Godhead?

It should be apparent that Jesus is not praying for our essential oneness. As I have argued, we already possess this spiritual oneness because all who know Christ participate in the divine nature (2 Peter 1:4). The oneness Jesus prayed for assumes this spiritual participation in his death and resurrection life and goes further to address the functional oneness I have referred to as *relational unity*—a oneness that is the expression of the eternal, spiritual unity of the Father and Son. During Jesus' earthly lifetime, this relational oneness is seen most clearly in his mediatorial role (see John 5:19, 36; 14:10). Though the Son is co-eternal and co-equal with the Father, in the Son's incarnation as Jesus of Nazareth he faithfully developed and expressed a relational unity with his Father each and every moment of his human life.

As Christians, we believe that the Holy Spirit lives in us. Because he indwells us, our lives become the sphere of his divine activity (cf. John 14:12; 15:1–17). Through the direct, daily work of God's Spirit in our lives, we experience a new vitality and freshness as we relate to one another and to God. God is truly at work in our lives and we can see the evidence of his activity and work. As those entrusted with carrying forward God's mission, our unity with him involves both human and divine cooperation. To experience this unity, we must live in constant dependence on God and express a humble willingness to embrace his will and his purposes.

LOVE IS THE CENTER

As we saw in the last chapter, the love of God is the greatest force in the entire universe. "God *is* love" (1 John 4:8, italics added). The love of God is central to who God is, and this love is reflected in the unity of the divine life: "I and the Father are one" (John 10:30). This divine unity is also a unity of redemptive purpose (John 17:20–26). The love of God for the world is demonstrated in the giving of his Son to save the world from the consequences of sin. We reciprocate God's loving initiative as we offer ourselves to him in heartfelt surrender: "We love because he first loved us" (1 John 4:19).

These phrases can seem remote and sentimental if we lack the relational unity that underlies them. This love that God has for us and the love we have for him are intended to be visibly expressed through our actions: "Let us not love with words or tongue but with actions and in truth" (1 John 3:18). In fact, the entire will of God can be effectively summarized in two commands: We are to love God and our neighbors (Luke 10:27). Love and active obedience to God's will go hand in hand. As Jesus plainly said, "If you love me, keep my commands" (John 14:15).

Some have suggested that the apostle John limits the love of God to the Christian community. Rather than argue over the details, I simply suggest that Christ's fellowship with his disciples is the place where the love of God is most openly displayed. If "God is love," then our expressions of love within the Christian community must line up with his. It is his love that enlarges our hearts and forms our character so that we are freed to love others, whether they are a fellow Christian or an enemy.

COOPERATIONAL LOVE

If God's love is at the center of church life and is an expression of the spiritual unity of the Trinity and our inclusion in Christ, then we are compelled to consider how we can work together in Christ's mission. Relational unity with Christ should lead us to embrace a cooperational unity with other Christians. Now I understand that the word *cooperational* instantly frightens some people. Some will think that cooperation is synonymous with compromise—that by working together we are somehow selling out our beliefs and watering down our convictions. I find that those who approach relationships within the body of Christ with an attitude of suspicion and fear have little likelihood of experiencing the relational love Jesus encourages us to have for one another.

Let's explore three ways to think about this type of cooperational unity, based on the words of Jesus in John 17.

UNANIMITY

Unanimity assumes we should reach agreement in everything. This is the tendency of some Catholics, given their belief about the **magisterium** and the **papacy**. Professor Hans Küng, a Catholic theologian who has often criticized his own church, correctly concludes:

> The unity of the church is not simply a natural unity, is not simply a moral unanimity and harmony, is not just sociological conformity and uniformity. To judge it by externals (canon law, ecclesiastical language, church administration, etc.) is to misunderstand it completely. The unity of the church is a spiritual entity. It is not chiefly a unity of members among

> themselves, it depends finally not on itself but on the unity
> of God, which is efficacious through Jesus Christ in the Holy
> Spirit. . . . It is one and the same confession of faith in the
> Lord Jesus, the same hope of blessedness, the same love,
> which is experienced in oneness of heart, the same ser-
> vice of the world. The church *is* one and therefore *should*
> *be* one.[4]

Liberal Protestants have tended to move in the opposite direction and see agreement on any significant doctrinal formulation as
nonessential. The Eastern Orthodox Church generally navigates
this question differently than Western Christians, arguing for a
unanimity rooted in the earliest creeds and their liturgy—without
a magisterium or pope.

The issue of unanimity comes down to this: Can there be real
disciples who understand one or more points of doctrine in ways
that appear contrary to your tradition? I am convinced that a truly
evangelical approach—one solidly rooted in the good news of
Jesus Christ (**kerygma**)—can endure different understandings on
many doctrinal issues. I think about it this way: we allow for sin in
other people and make room for weak or misguided Christians. In
much the way we hold to the idea of *simul justus et peccator* (we are
"simultaneously righteous and sinful"), why can we not embrace
the corresponding idea of *simul fidelis et incredulous*—that we are
both believers and unbelievers at one and the same time. If we
are honest, every one of us at some point in our lives confesses,
"Lord, I do believe; help me overcome my unbelief."

Thinking of it in this way helps me understand why in the best
of churches, as well as in the worst, you will always find people
who truly love Jesus. As I realize this, I am delivered from the drive
to pursue perfect unanimity on every matter of faith, while allow-
ing me to continue to care deeply about doctrine.

UNIFORMITY

In the history of the church, *uniformity* in faith and practice has
been the default approach when ritual and liturgical practices
are made central. There is much to commend in this approach.
This view, almost unknown in modern American churches, unites
Christians around a common liturgical practice that allows the

whole church to worship and practice the faith together. While it can lead to the problem of ritualism, it can also create a deep sense of unity among believers.

In the private prep school I attended, we all were required to wear a uniform. Because we all dressed the same way, I never had to think about what to wear. Some may argue that this requirement created too much uniformity at the school, but I can assure you it had a different effect on me. It gave me a calm confidence about my appearance that allowed me to focus my energy and attention on more important matters. I remained an individual, but I was part of a group in which unity was demonstrated through what we wore. The wearing of a uniform had a positive impact on my studies.

That said, I will acknowledge that uniformity in the Christian church can lead to serious problems, especially as Christ's mission takes root in various and diverse cultures. How does the gospel, a historical message given within a specific culture, adapt to new cultures? How do we "become all things to all people so that by all possible means [we] might save some" (1 Corinthians 9:22)? The church must become a missional community that is culturally inclusive and doctrinally strong. Attempts to create ecclesial uniformity sometimes fail this missional test when a particular culture becomes too closely identified with the truth.

UNION

Union emphasizes the goal of Jesus' prayer—to bring all of us into one visible, united church. Most Catholics and Orthodox Christians believe that union is essential to true unity, but this view creates a huge barrier as they try to address the historic East/West divide in the church.

Nothing seemed to break the heart of the late Pope John Paul II more than the breakdown of talks about unity with the Orthodox Church. (He referred to the whole church as having two lungs—East and West). Part of the reason for the breakdown was the way each group understood the notion of union. The papacy, which is at the center of the unity issue for Catholics, presents a serious problem for other Christians.

I frequently use the term *union* to refer to what happens when several churches unite together (reconcile). Union took place in South India during the twentieth century, and it takes place regularly in local communities when several churches unite to form one congregation. In a global sense, we may be farther from this kind of union than we've ever been in Christian history.

Other expressions of union are found among the common accords that have allowed certain Protestant communions to enter into ministerial relationships across their divides. More conservative Protestants have often feared unions, believing that they require serious doctrinal compromise. Typically, the crux of these debates has been the place and ministry of the Lord's Supper.

Most scholars agree that very little in the New Testament resembles anything like a central church that represented all Christian churches. In the book of Acts, particularly at the Council of Jerusalem (Acts 15:1–29), we do find a limited expression of union. Acts 15 shows us how several leaders of different churches came together to reach an agreement based on a minimal set of conclusions aimed at preserving their oneness in mission. Considering the very real danger of false teaching and doctrinal error, the agreement is rather shocking in terms of how far they were willing to go to make sure that the gospel spread freely and the church remained undivided. That said, formal structures and plans for organizational union between churches really have little to do with what we read about in Acts 15.

None of these understandings of unity — unanimity, uniformity, and union — truly fit the context of the New Testament. The aim of the early church was the evangelization of the world. The purpose of their oneness was to be a visible representation of God's love.

WHAT MEANS DO WE HAVE FOR COOPERATION?

The Scriptures teach us that Christ gives us his divine life through the gift of the Holy Spirit — the "bond of love," according to Augustine. The earliest creeds put the doctrine of the church and its oneness in the section on the Holy Spirit.

All Christians "participate in the [mystery of the] divine nature" (2 Peter 1:3–4), and our participation in this mystery is an important way in which we pursue our relational unity in Christ (2 Corinthians 3:18; Hebrews 12:10; 1 John 3:2). Our common participation in the divine nature means that Christians should never conceive of life in community apart from Christ. All of the riches of the Godhead are found in Christ, and these riches are now ours through our union with him. Pardon, righteousness, love, joy, wisdom, kindness, gentleness, and tenderness are found in him. And they are now at work in us by the Holy Spirit's power. This is the key to biblical unity and our concern for the next chapter—keeping the focus on Christ as the center.

QUESTIONS FOR DISCUSSION AND REFLECTION

1. How might our unity serve as a witness to non-Christians? Can you think of an example of how this might happen?

2. What does the unity of the Trinity have to do with our unity with each other as Christians?

3. How is church unity an expression of God's love? What does this mean in your particular context?

4. Consider the three types of unity that have been offered as an explanation for what Jesus meant in John 17:20–23. What are the strengths and weaknesses of each one?

chapter six

Christ the Center

Only in Christ are all things in communion. He is the point of convergence of all hearts and beings and therefore the bridge and the shortest way from each to each.

Hans Urs von Balthasar

AS WE LOOKED AT HOW JESUS PRAYED for unity among all his disciples, we discovered that this unity is based on the relational and cooperational communion that existed between the Father and the Son during his earthly ministry. This divine unity between the Father and the Son forms the basis for our own experience of unity with other Christians. But how is our experience of unity, as followers of Christ, bound up with the success of Christ's mission?

The late Roman Catholic theologian Raymond E. Brown provides helpful insight in his exposition of John 17:

> As in [John] 10:16, believers (evangelized by different disciples) are not one flock, but unity is prayed for. Vital contact with this future generation and all subsequent generations will not be lost, for Jesus will dwell in them. The indwelling of Jesus, the Christian's earthly share in eternal life, provides the great bond of union connecting Christians of all times with the Father. Jesus' love for them is the same as his love for his immediate disciples: a love patterned on the eternal love of the Father for the Son. (So perfect is this love that it will force even the world's recognition!) And they too shall have a share in the eternal glory of the Son.[1]

Christian believers have lived in different nations, cultural contexts, and ethnic settings since the middle of the first century. They have spoken a myriad of languages and have worshiped the triune God in diverse ways. Yet in Christ they remain one people because there is only one flock and one shepherd. Expressions of this one communion may vary, but Christ remains at the center. The issue of whether or not the whole church should be visibly organized will continue to be discussed and debated. But this much is true: we are spiritually one, not two or three.

My understanding of biblical oneness combines two commitments that are often considered separately. The first is a commitment to work in every conceivable way to demonstrate and express the God-given spiritual oneness I share with other believers through our union with Christ. This means a willingness to work with the Christians I know and with those I don't know well. It includes my closest friends and family members as well as churches halfway around the world. Whether people are a part of my church communion or another — Catholic, Protestant, or Orthodox — I begin by recognizing I am one with them in Christ if they call him Lord (1 Corinthians 12:3). Growing in biblical oneness with other believers begins with a commitment to aggressively pursue specific ways to demonstrate our common love for Christ.

But my second commitment goes even further. Many Protestant evangelicals are satisfied with informal person-to-person expressions of oneness. Because they tend to view the church as a voluntary association, they see no need to seek unity with other churches. I believe the pursuit of oneness means we must not shy away from opportunities to engage in relational and cooperational unity between churches — Protestant, Catholic, and Orthodox. Though the three great historic branches of the Christian church cannot presently pursue union with one another, they *can* seek greater relational and cooperational unity even as they pray for ways to address the historic differences that have led to disunity in the past. We must never settle just for personal oneness with other individuals. The pursuit of biblical oneness embraces a concern for the unity of the wider church as well. I personally pray every single day that this would become a reality between churches, locally and globally.

I am often asked, "Do you think the great divided churches will ever become one church?" I often respond by asking, "Who can possibly know what God will do in the centuries ahead?" Could people from centuries past have foreseen what has transpired in the last century? For hundreds of years, Catholics and Protestants were fierce enemies. Entire nations and families were divided. Bloody wars were fought over these differences. Following the Council of Trent in the sixteenth century and Vatican Council I in the late nineteenth century, no one could have predicted what would happen in the twentieth century. What might happen in the twenty-first or twenty-second century, if Christ has not returned? Who can know what the Spirit will do as the world grows smaller and the church grows larger? What will happen in Africa, where the fast-growing church and the fast-spreading religion of Islam exist side by side?

Perhaps the most important question, though, relates to Christ's mission: How will God finally accomplish his purpose to save a people from "every tribe and language and people and nation" (Revelation 5:9)? Though I see no obvious reason to say the church must become organizationally united, I do believe we will see and experience unprecedented relational unity when Christ finally returns and his prayer is fully answered. If the answer to this prayer is certain, what might happen prior to Christ's return? Will the Spirit lead us to embrace unity, bringing us closer to the final consummation?

Already we see evidence for the spread of a Spirit-given unity that defies our old categories of division. I welcome all serious interactions between churches and individuals who want to pursue the supremacy of Christ together. If Christ is truly the center, then we can move toward him and find fellowship with one another in the process.

This two-commitment approach may seem obvious to those who love the church. But it has practical consequences for those who consider themselves evangelicals. It means I can no longer be an anti-Catholic, evangelical (Reformed) Protestant. With deep conviction, I am compelled to regard both Catholics and the Catholic Church with love and esteem. This personal commitment to oneness has enabled me to draw great blessings from the

Catholic tradition and develop many wonderful friendships with Catholic brothers and sisters in Christ.

OUR SENSE OF ONENESS

For the first thousand years of its history, the church universally maintained an interest in unity. However, in 1054, this unity was radically and tragically altered by the East/West split. Centuries later, the Protestant Reformation broke the Catholic Church's unity in Europe. The events that followed produced new visible church communions in Germany, Great Britain, the Netherlands, and Switzerland. Among Protestants, the Anabaptists and the various Free Church movements further divided the visible church. While both sides of the sixteenth-century debate initially tried to preserve the unity of the church, each side made decisions that would eventually make this all but impossible (at least for the next five centuries).

As I studied this era of Western history, I discovered a virtually unknown story. Leaders on both sides found compelling reasons to preserve unity even as the church was being divided. For many of the leaders of the Reformation, division was never seen as a desirable result. But as the rhetoric increased and the conflict grew more intense over time, deep divisions developed. Since the sixteenth century, countless church splits have only deepened the chasms between churches.

Still, an amazing reality points to the ongoing work of God in the church. Despite these tragic schisms, there remains a deep desire for unity within the hearts of many Protestants and Catholics. The Protestant theologian G. W. Bromiley expresses this sense of oneness:

> [The church] has been split by innumerable dissensions and disagreements. It has passed through many crises and vicissitudes. It has known ages of the most violent individualism as well as the most submissive collectivism. But for all the legitimate or illegitimate variety it has never lost its ultimate and indestructible unity.[2]

The ground of this undeniable sense of oneness is found in the Bible. In the Old Testament, the Jews were the people of

God. They were not *two* peoples, but *one* people. Even though they were divided into twelve tribes and later became two different kingdoms, they still remained *one* chosen people descended from *one* man. When they left Egypt, they left as *one* people, and when God gave them his law, it was not a law for many nations and groups but a divine treasure for *one* people. Yes, they fought civil wars and turned on each other at times, but in the end nothing could destroy the inherent oneness Israel experienced when she remembered her divine origins and the one covenant that united her.

The New Testament does not alter this principle of unity as a characteristic of God's people. The church consists of people from every tribe, nation, and language, but all of them find their fundamental identity in *one* person—Jesus Christ. This principle—of the one and the many—is rooted in the communal nature of God as Trinity. The ethnic ground of unity, as seen in the Old Testament arrangement, has passed away. In its place we find the spiritual unity of the new covenant—a new unity rooted in *one* Savior, whose death and resurrection give birth to *one* organism, the church. For this reason, Bromiley has concluded, "The whole structure of the New Testament church, or churches, shows us that there is a strong and indissoluble sense of unity not only with the local congregation but extending to the church as a whole."[3] We should never become complacent about the disunity of God's people. We must cultivate a holy discontent about our unholy divisions.

When Israel under the old order was brought to an end, it was not destroyed but was fulfilled in the new covenant. (This doesn't mean ethnic Israel has no place in the plan of God [see Romans 11] and certainly doesn't justify any form of anti-Semitism). What emerged from the old covenant was something in continuity with the holy intentions of God for his one people. The unity once confined to a single ethnic people is now a spiritual reality—"a "holy nation, God's special possession" (1 Peter 2:9) that is inherently one, since Christ is the Lord of the church and Christians are brought into his church through faith in him. As Christians, true spiritual unity is the oneness we experience as we are drawn to Christ together.

The Old Testament was the Bible of the early church, and it taught that there could be only one temple of God, not two or three. But the writers of the New Testament Scriptures taught that the one temple was now a new temple. The church of God is made up of "living stones" that are built into a "spiritual house"—a new temple where we collectively offer spiritual sacrifices to God (1 Peter 2:5). If Christians are to truly live out the reality of this one (spiritual) temple of God, then there is no place for rival, competing movements. There is one "place" where we worship—the mercy seat of Christ. Christ is also the cornerstone of the new temple, with the apostles—their teaching and witness—as the foundation. As followers of Christ, we are the blocks that make up this living temple, fitted together by God, the architect and builder of his church (see 1 Corinthians 3:16–17; 2 Corinthians 6:16; Ephesians 2:21–22; Hebrews 3:6).

CHRIST THE CENTER

I find it helpful to think of the worldwide church as a large circle. At the center of this circle is Christ. As people on the outer edge of the circle move inward toward Christ at the center, they grow closer to one another. This Christ-centered unity is not found in man-made structures or efforts to achieve oneness. It is the fruit of our nearness to Christ and is modeled on the unity that Christ experienced with the Father. It is a *relational* unity, experienced and revealed through shared mission.

Ignatius of Antioch once said that where Jesus Christ was, there you saw the catholic church. The theologian Jürgen Moltmann adds to this idea and suggests that the church is present wherever "the manifestation of the Spirit" resides.[4] The British theologian P. T. Forsyth rightly contends that the unity of the church lies "not in itself but in its message, in the unity of the gospel that made the church."[5] In some sense, all of these views are correct. The incarnate person of Christ, the indwelling presence of the Spirit in the hearts of believers, and the proclamation of the gospel message are all essential characteristics of the relational unity that defines the oneness of the church.

The German martyr-theologian Dietrich Bonhoeffer has sometimes been viewed as a radical who wanted to do away with the "religious elements" of the church. But Bonhoeffer remained a faithful Lutheran to his final day. He rightly stressed that the *who* question—our identity—must always come before the *what* question—our practice: When I know *who* the person is who does this, I will also know *what* he does. His stress was always on the Christ who came before the church, on the Christ who judges the church, and on the Christ who stands at the center of the church. His famous lectures of 1933 bear the title *Christ the Center.*

In later chapters we will consider mission as a key component of our unity, but at this point it is crucial to remember that true unity always begins with the question, Who is Jesus Christ? Only by beginning with the person of Jesus can Christians develop a serious approach to unity, since our unity is found *in Christ alone*, not in the visible structures or particular practices of individual churches. In this sense, Bonhoeffer was right. If we are to pursue unity, especially in the church of the future, we must begin with Christ at the center![6]

QUESTIONS FOR DISCUSSION AND REFLECTION

1. Do you believe there is only one church? If so, what does it mean to you? How does it affect your understanding of your local church and its witness?

2. If there is only one church and Jesus is Lord of that church, what should your response be to schism and division? How should you deal with personal disagreements that you have with other believers and churches?

3. How does the growth and development of the church in the non-Western nations impact you? How can the church in the West respond to these changes?

4. How can you make sure that Christ is at the center of all you are and do?

chapter seven

The Four Classical Marks of the Church

In the Catholic Church itself, all possible care must be taken that we hold that faith which has been believed everywhere, always, by all.

Vincent of Lerins

You did not first learn the Lord's Prayer and after that the Creed; but first the Creed, from which you should know what to believe, and afterward the Lord's Prayer, from which you should know whom to invoke. The Creed outlines the articles of faith, whereas the Lord's Prayer tells you how to address your petitions; because it is the man of faith that has his prayers heard.

Saint Augustine

WHEN I FIRST BEGAN TO REFLECT deeply on the words of the two great early creeds (the Apostles' Creed and the Nicene Creed), I was brought face-to-face with a word that deeply troubled me: *catholic*.[1] I now believe this one word is so important that it is difficult to remain faithful to orthodoxy without embracing it. The reasons for its importance lie in its use by early Christians and its meaning in the classical Christian tradition.

ANTI-CATHOLICISM

When I first began to struggle with the historical understanding of catholicity, I came to see how deeply anti-Catholic I had been for most of my life. Even using the word *catholic* with a small *c* disturbed me. Thinking back to my childhood and the 1960 presidential election, I recall my pastor telling the congregation why Christians should not vote for Senator John F. Kennedy. A Kennedy presidency would allow the papacy to have too much influence in America.

I first used the word *catholic* in a church that recited the Apostles' Creed. I felt safe using it in this context, but I soon discovered that many of the members didn't understand the creed, even though they said it every week. One elder even confessed that he never said the word *catholic* aloud when he recited the words.

Much of my struggle was the product of my own fears. To counter my fear, I decided to dig deeper to try to understand why the church had chosen to express its faith through the centuries in these words from the Nicene Creed: "one holy catholic and apostolic" church. Traditionally, these key words are known as the four "marks" of the church. Let's unpack each and see what they show us about the understanding of unity in the early church.

THE CHURCH IS ONE

When we say that the church is one, we are making a statement that is clearly consistent with apostolic testimony: "There is one body" (Ephesians 4:4). This idea of *oneness* should be taken in at least two senses.

First, it implies *uniqueness*. There is nothing else like the church. This sense of a unique status can be wrongly abused when advanced as a claim of privilege over and against another group of people—for example, when people refer to themselves as the "favored" people of God, or the "one true church throughout all history." If this notion of uniqueness becomes too prominent, as it has in some polemics, then we begin to insist that salvation is found *only in our church*. The Catholic scholar Luke Timothy Johnson notes that though there is a "certain truth to the ideal of a single church, it is [nonetheless] an ideal that, when claimed as a reality, can become dangerous."[2]

I do believe we can claim uniqueness for the church in reference to our common salvation in Christ. The church is made up of everyone who "calls on the name of the Lord" (Romans 10:13;

1 Corinthians 1:2). But the uniqueness of our common identity is abused when it only refers to our narrow understanding of who belongs among God's people.

The second way we can understand *oneness* is to see it as an ideal to be pursued. In this sense, the church is one because there is "one body and one Spirit, ... one hope...; one Lord, one faith, one baptism; one God and Father of all" (Ephesians 4:4–6). Yet the oneness of the church does not negate the rich diversity of its individual members. Instead, the oneness of the church is characteristic of its mission and identity as a body that unites diverse people together. The spiritual unity that exists among those who belong to Christ must still be visibly manifest among them. Thus, observes Johnson, "Paul sees ... that unity is not the same thing as uniformity. Indeed the unity of the Spirit allows and even requires diversity. The diversity within the community is analogous to the trinity of persons within the one God."[3] The United States Conference of Catholic Bishops adds, "The church of the twenty-first century will be, as it has always been, a church of many cultures, languages, and traditions, yet simultaneously one, as God is one—Father, Son, and Holy Spirit—unity in diversity."[4]

THE CHURCH IS HOLY

God's command to Israel was very clear: "Be holy, because I am holy" (Leviticus 11:45). This command, in the context of the covenant, was for all of Israel, not simply for select individuals. God's holiness made him "other," and he commanded his people to be "other" than the world around them. The New Testament also emphasizes this concept of corporate holiness (1 Corinthians 1:2; 6:11; Ephesians 5:26; 1 Thessalonians 4:3, 7). There is an ongoing tension in the New Testament between what we already are in Christ and what we are urged to become in actual practice (1 Corinthians 1:2; 2 Corinthians 7:1; 1 Thessalonians 3:13; 4:3). Though the church is the holy temple of God, it must also express holiness in its actual behavior, albeit imperfectly, through dependence on God's sustaining and transforming grace (1 Corinthians 6:19–20).

Luke Timothy Johnson argues that holiness has been understood in two specific ways in the church—*ritually* and *morally*. Debates over ritual forms of worship have resulted in division, and debates about what constitutes proper moral practice continue to divide the church. How can we determine which ethical practices are normative for Christians? Johnson writes:

> The impulse toward holiness in the church has tended toward disunity.... Some Christians insist that obedience to the pope is a betrayal of the obedience of faith that is owed only to the gospel, others that the obedience to the pope is the perfect expression of obedience to the gospel. Some Christians separate from others (or drive others out) over the time and style of baptism, the nature of the Eucharist, the need (or not) of bishops, how the Scripture is to be read, who is to be ordained, and many other "essentials."[5]

From the Montanists to the Marcionites, the Hutterites to the Holiness Pentecostals, the biblical call to holiness has often created division. In light of the long history of division caused by different understandings of what is morally right and wrong for Christians, it seems fair to ask, "Is it really possible to both pursue corporate holiness as a church and preserve unity?" Recognizing the diversity of ways in which Christians have understood and responded to the call to holy living is a good starting point. But recognizing that Christians have had different perspectives on this issue doesn't settle the problems that continue to threaten our unity. I am persuaded that there are no easy solutions. Still, we must recognize that holiness, both as a spiritual reality and as a mark of actual practice in the lives of believers, is an essential characteristic of the church.

THE CHURCH IS CATHOLIC

The creeds tell us that that church is catholic. Some argue this is simply another way of saying that it is universal. Some churches have even chosen to change the creed, replacing *catholic* with *Christian*. This not only weakens our understanding of the term *catholic*; it's redundant. The church is inherently Christian. There is no other way of defining the church.

The Greek word *katholikos* literally means "throughout the whole world." Luke Timothy Johnson suggests that the true sense of the word is nuanced by both universality and inclusiveness:

"As applied in the creed to the ideal church, it means both a universality of extent and an inclusiveness that embraces differences within a larger unity."[6] Note carefully that while the notion of universality is true, it does not convey the fullness of what is meant by catholicity. Johnson comments,

> The creed does not say that the church is "Roman Catholic." That term is, indeed, oxymoronic. It combines the element of universality with a highly particular adjective. The Roman Catholic tradition (the reader will remember it is my own) may believe the Roman tradition is all-encompassing, but that is simply mistaken.[7]

I believe that recovering a proper understanding of the term *catholic* is extremely important for future unity. What is at stake is a reality that the creed has underscored for millions of confessing Christians for two thousand years. The notion of catholicity in the creed tells us that the church is universal in its extent and that it embraces a unity that goes beyond local and personal differences. The word *catholic* reminds us that this community extends across the globe and through time, incorporating all of the redeemed throughout the ages.

Johnson advocates for retaining the word because "the catholic church is the one that exists everywhere, rather than simply in one place. Implicitly, then, catholicity asserts the general over the particular in any argument about the nature of the church."[8] This gets at the idea of *inclusiveness*. Many of our historic denominations, as well as many of the smaller and more energetic evangelical fellowships, tend to be defined more by things such as ethnicity, views about gender, and partisan politics than by a common confession of salvation through the grace offered in Christ. But Jesus offered table fellowship to a wide array of sinners and openly associated with all "the wrong people." The word *catholic* keeps us rooted in our historical and confessional past and requires that we reject any exclusiveness as well as unbiblical requirements that keep people from our fellowship that are not germane to the good news.

The word *catholic* also corrects the tendency of Christians to speak in ways that tend to emphasize the **mystical** unity of the church in a way that ignores or minimizes the real, human church.

Francis Schaeffer expressed it well: "We make a mockery of what Jesus is saying [John 13:33–35; 17:21] unless we understand that he is talking about something visible."[9] In our discussions about the catholic church, we must always keep in mind that the church is something that really exists—with real, fallible human beings—and is not just a concept or an idea.

THE CHURCH IS APOSTOLIC

The Nicene Creed adds a fourth word about the Spirit's ministry: the church is **apostolic**. The church is intimately and historically linked with the apostles. This truth has also been primarily understood in two ways.

First, in order to combat the ancient error of **Gnosticism**, fathers of the church such as Irenaeus and Tertullian made continuity with the apostles an essential mark of the church. Roman Catholic and Orthodox Christians came to believe that a line of historical succession from the apostles to the present was necessary and evident in their respective traditions. For believers in these traditions, the apostolicity of the church means more than just the scriptural witness, though this is not always so precisely stated. Churches that embrace the understanding of apostolic succession believe that the apostolic teaching of the church includes the interpretations offered by the church councils, especially those decisions formulated during the first eight centuries. Admittedly, there is no simple way of reconciling the differing perspectives on what defines apostolic authority. However, much progress is being made through the serious study of the **patristic** writings and a better grasp of the teachings of the early church.

That said, I believe there is a better way to understand the word *apostolic*. Luke Timothy Johnson expresses it well:

> The church in every age must be measured by the standard of the apostolic age as witnessed not by the later tradition but by direct appeal to the writings of the New Testament. Placing the contemporary church against the one depicted in the Acts of the Apostles makes clear how much the prophetic witness of the church has been compromised by its many strategies of adaptation and survival over the centuries. This is the sense of the word employed by reformers like

> Martin Luther, who combated the excrescences of medieval Catholicism by appealing to the teaching and practice of the New Testament. Where in the New Testament do we find pope or cardinals? Where do we find mandatory celibacy? Where do we find indulgences, or even purgatory? Where do we find the office of the Inquisition? These are powerful questions. Equally needed is the prophetic call to a simpler and more radical "New Testament" lifestyle by Christians.[10]

A healthy concern for apostolicity reminds us that we need to constantly reexamine our practices and structures in light of the apostolic practice of the early church. This fourth mark reminds all of us, especially those who do not believe in apostolic succession, that we must take the historical witness of the church seriously. We need fresh reminders that our culture-specific manifestations of church must undergo the constant critique of the Scriptures.

Still, a mistaken emphasis on apostolicity can sometimes result in denying legitimate forms of the Spirit's work in the present age as we search for the "perfect" expression of the church. Johnson concludes, "The prophetic voice can all too easily be just as reflexively hostile to institution and authority as authority and institution are reflexively hostile to the voice of prophecy."[11]

Raymond Brown once noted that the kind of institutional authority that attempts to drive an opinion or idea out the front door of the church will often allow it to enter through the back door a generation later. The apostolic nature of the church reminds us that every generation needs fresh reminders of our origins, while still looking for innovative ways to engage our contemporary context.

TENSION AND CONFLICT

Tension and conflict in relationships are all too common. We've all experienced them at one time or another. Struggles that one married couple works through and survives may end up dividing another. Over time, I have noticed that people tend to stay in relationships and work through their differences when they love each other deeply and are committed to finding solutions.

In the church, we who claim to love Christ must be committed to staying together in our relationships with other believers. After four decades of ministry, having spoken and consulted with well over a thousand churches, I've noticed that most divisions in the church are not because of a major doctrinal disagreement; they are the result of a breakdown in our love for one another. When love grows cold, it isn't too hard to find a "cause" that allows us to justify breaking fellowship with someone. Often, divisions result simply because we lack the patience to "carry each other's burdens" and "fulfill the law of Christ" (Galatians 6:2).

The four historical marks of the church are great reminders of a classical Christian perspective on unity. While these marks will not solve all our disagreements (we can even disagree on how to interpret them), they do provide us with a reliable setting in which to develop a common understanding of what it means to be the church.

QUESTIONS FOR DISCUSSION AND REFLECTION

1. How would you describe anti-Catholicism? Do you see this spirit in your life or in your church? What can be done to correct it?

2. In what way are the four marks important for you and your church? Do they matter to you? Why or why not? How would you teach these marks to those who do not understand them?

3. What brings about conflicts within your church? Have you ever experienced a church split or division? What could have been done to prevent it? What should you do now to prevent it from happening again?

4. How can the persecuted church help us understand Christian unity in our own context? What are the merits of talking more openly about suffering and its role in our holiness and oneness?

present

RESTORING UNITY IN
THE CHURCH TODAY

chapter eight

How Can We Restore Unity?

The blessed apostle John distinguished no heresy or schism, neither did he set down any as specially separated, but he called all who had gone out from the church, and who acted in opposition to the church, antichrist.

Cyprian

The doctrine of justification is in fact the great ecumenical doctrine.

N. T. Wright

I HAVE ARGUED that the early church held an extremely high view of oneness and catholicity. We do not have to search far to understand why: "There is one body and one Spirit, just as you were called to one hope when you were called; one Lord, one faith, one baptism; one God and Father of all, who is over all and through all and in all" (Ephesians 4:4–6).

The ancient Jewish people, the recipients of God's covenant promises, were continually assured that God's purpose was to use their witness to spread the knowledge of God to all the peoples of the earth. This idea is clearly seen in the initial announcement of the covenant God made with Abraham: "I will bless those who bless you, and whoever curses you I will curse; and all peoples on earth will be blessed through you" (Genesis 12:3). God later told Abraham he intended for him to be "the father of many nations" (17:4).

The Old Testament prophets repeatedly reminded the people that this covenantal purpose had never been forgotten by God.

God's universal, worldwide plan was to spread his glory throughout the whole earth. Thus Isaiah wrote, "The earth will be filled
with the knowledge of the LORD as the waters cover the sea"
(Isaiah 11:9).

When you read the earliest Christian writers, you immediately see how clearly they understood this one divine purpose. In
time, they believed that God's eternal purpose was to be fulfilled
through the church. The fulfillment of God's covenant promise to
Abraham made the church catholic—scattered throughout the
whole earth—as the gospel message went out to the Gentile
nations.

The catholicity of the church means that God's people are
scattered throughout time and across the earth. Is it even possible, given these differences, for us to restore a sense of unity
to the divided modern church?

THE APOSTLES' CREED CAN HELP US

The Apostles' Creed is the earliest summary of the teaching of
Christian faith in the postapostolic era. This creed arranges the
essential truths of the Christian faith in a natural and logical pro-
gression. The order of divine revelation, consciously rooted in
the persons of the Trinity, is carefully followed. The creed moves
from God the Father and his creation to the person and work
of Christ—his supernatural birth, life, death, and resurrection.
Then it brings us to the Holy Spirit—the church and the future.
The great nineteenth-century Protestant theologian Philip Schaff
speaks of the unique characteristics of the creed:

> It is by far the best popular summary of the Christian faith
> ever made within so brief a space. It still surpasses all later
> symbols for catechetical and liturgical purposes, especially
> as a profession of candidates for baptism and church mem-
> bership. It is not a logical statement of abstract doctrines,
> but a profession of living facts and saving truths. It is a
> liturgical poem and an act of worship. Like the Lord's Prayer,
> it loses none of its charm and effect by frequent use, al-
> though, by vain and thoughtless repetition, it may be made
> a martyr and an empty form of words. It is intelligible and
> edifying to a child, and fresh and rich to the profoundest

Christian scholar, who, as he advances in age, delights to go back to primitive foundations and first principles. It has the fragrance of antiquity and the inestimable weight of universal consent. It is a bond of union between all ages and sections of Christendom. It can never be superseded for popular use in church and school.[1]

Augustine (AD 354–430) referred to the Apostles' Creed "as a brief and grand regulator of true faith." Martin Luther believed that the Christian truth could not be put into a shorter and clearer statement. John Calvin, who followed the order of the Apostles' Creed as he arranged his *Institutes of the Christian Religion*, believed that this creed was an admirable and true summary of the Christian faith. The famous Lutheran J. T. Müller said that the creed held "the double significance" of being both a bond of union for the universal church and the seed from which all other creeds have grown. And the Reformed theologian W. G. T. Shedd, writing in the nineteenth century, saw the Apostles' Creed as the earliest attempt by Christian minds to systematize the teachings of Scripture. He called the creed "the uninspired foundation" on which the whole superstructure of symbolic literature rests. What more can I say?

The Apostles' Creed is a dynamic treasure. When we fail to utilize it as a basic guide for teaching the essentials of our faith, we practically invite disunity. Those who ignore the creed are generally left to focus on the truths they prefer to major on rather than the essential beliefs that have been universally believed and taught by all Christians.

We find no other document in early church history, apart from the Bible, that served a greater purpose in uniting Christians in their common faith. The creed was confessed in one's baptism, affirmed regularly by the whole gathered church, and openly used to express the kind of essential Christianity that united believers. The Apostles' Creed has the pride of place in history as well as the clarity of true simplicity. There is plenty in it that offends the sensibilities of modern culture, making it the perfect ancient-future way of establishing fidelity and unity.

In the early church, this creed provided a rather explicit response to three challenges, summarized by Luke Timothy Johnson:

The first challenge was to define the experience of Jesus within and over against the shared story of Israel. The second challenge was to clarify the complex understanding of God that was embedded in the resurrection experiences. The third challenge was to correct misunderstandings of the newly emergent "Christian narrative" that was, at heart, a "story about Jesus."[2]

A CONFESSIONAL BASIS FOR TRUE CATHOLICITY

As I began to recognize the historical importance of the Apostles' Creed, I also saw how this statement could begin to shape our faith and practice. I had been taught to believe that the church should follow the Bible, never human creeds. In my church as a youth we had proudly declared, "We have no creed but the Bible." (I now think this is one of the most potentially divisive things a sincere Christian can utter.) Until I began studying the creed, I didn't realize just how wrong my thinking was about essential Christianity. I had no concern for catholicity and remained a separated Christian. I was even proud of my distinct beliefs! The creed, however, gave me a place to stand with my brothers and sisters without having to surrender my core orthodoxy.

Everyone interprets the Bible. This truth may be abundantly clear to you, but I have found that it is easily forgotten by "Bible-centered" Christians. Quoting the Bible rarely settles disagreements. By themselves, Bible verses fail to promote unity. Consider the fact that many cults will affirm the inerrancy and authority of the Bible, yet they interpret its meaning in ways that suit their own personal preference. In truth, we need to have a way of grasping the answer to a larger question: What is the *essential* message of the Holy Scriptures?

Answering this question takes us back to the Bible as our foundation of truth, but it also incorporates the faithful witness of the ancient church. We ask such questions as: What did the first Christians believe and why did they believe it? How did they hear the gospel? Before there was a completed Bible, how did the church understand and confess the living message of Christ? (Even when the church had the completed Scriptures, most Christians never had the opportunity to read them, much less study them.) How has the church heard the Scriptures down through the ages? Questions such as these lead us to a study of history, an area of study known as historical theology, covering the church's understanding of the development of theology and its interpretation of the Scriptures over the past two thousand years. We never stand alone when we read and interpret the Bible. With a grasp of history and tradition, we are able to read the sacred Scriptures in communion with the "one holy catholic and apostolic church."

Studying how the historical church understood the Scriptures greatly helped me, but it wasn't easy. I had to learn to humble myself and truly listen to other voices outside of my cultural and generational context. My teachers included Catholic, Protestant, and Orthodox Christians.

If it helps, think about it this way: Are you the first person to ever read the Bible and attempt to understand its message? Of course not. People before you wrestled with these same writings and expressed what they understood in plain language. They confessed a "core orthodoxy." They celebrated the "**Great Tradition**" — those elemental truths representing the theological consensus of the first thousand years of Christian history. Wisdom should lead us to listen to these early Christians before we try to work out some of the difficult issues we face today. In a very real sense, we must look to the past before we are adequately prepared to answer the challenges of the future.

As best we can tell, the church has been using the Apostles' Creed since about AD 215. The form we presently use is a later revision. The statements in the creed indicate how the earliest post-apostolic Christians understood sacred tradition and the teaching of the apostles. While no one claims that the apostles actually wrote the creed, all agree that it bears their name because it is universally believed to be a faithful summary of their teaching.

When core orthodoxy, as represented by the Apostles' Creed, is not of primary importance, the result will always be a small view of the church. Churches will tend to be driven by personalities. We see strong evidence that this type of Christianity has spread around the world to millions of Christians and churches that lack a solid grasp of core orthodoxy.

Often, people tell me that catholicity doesn't matter anymore. They argue that what matters most is right doctrine, and we get right doctrine by a proper exegesis of the Bible. These folks will sometimes go on to insist that their church is right since they *truly* follow the Bible. Yet in many cases their church is less than two generations old. (Incidentally, this provides one reason why really important doctrines [the Trinity, for example] are not practically important in many American churches—they are not understood historically.) Was everyone who taught the Bible before them simply wrong? Or worse yet, have there been no true Christians for the past two thousand years? This way of thinking raises the question: Does catholicity really matter anymore, particularly for the American church?

THE PRESENT AMERICAN REALITY

It has been said that there are more than 100 different families of churches and more than 250 distinct denominational groups in the United States. Some may wonder, "What's wrong with that? Aren't denominations a good thing?" Some commend the division in the church as a pluriform expression of the faith. But I find no solid biblical basis for this way of thinking. Yes, the reality of denominations and church splits has led American Christians to produce some of the largest churches in the world. And no nation has historically sent out more missionaries. But something about this pattern seems inherently wrong, especially when churches continue to separate from one another over issues of minor importance.

Scandals and heresies dilute our witness to a watching world, and the church in America grows spiritually weaker with each passing day.

The hymn writer Samuel Stone wrote "The Church's One Foundation" (1865). A portion of one stanza paints a sad but accurate picture of the current American church:

> Though, with a scornful wonder
> Men see her sore oppressed,
> By schisms rent asunder,
> By heresies distressed.

Others are more optimistic. Sabine Baring-Gould, who wrote the hymn "Onward Christian Soldiers," included a not-so-well-known line in his hymn:

> We are not divided,
> All one body we,
> One in hope, in doctrine,
> One in charity.

Not quite a portrait of the actual reality, is it? A more honest version was composed by the late Robert McAfee Brown in his book *The Spirit of Protestantism* (1961): "We are all divided, not one body we, one lacks faith, another hope, and all lack charity."

Divisions plague the American church. We are "rent asunder" by schism, thus we are not "all one body." But I do not think the real problem has anything to do with denominations (I will address this in chapter 14.) Our real problem is sectarianism (which I will address in chapter 10). Sectarianism creates an attitude of exclusivity. And when we hold this attitude, we act as if we belong to a superior (understood as the best, right, only, pure) church. Indirectly, we claim to be closest to Christ. In some cases we even think to ourselves, "We are his body, and you _____ are not—at least not nearly as much as we are!" Our pride and arrogance minimize the faith of other Christians and work against the very catholicity we see evident in the New Testament church.

SATAN HATES A UNIFIED CHURCH

It's hard to miss the emphasis the early church placed on catholicity. Quotations that reinforce this characteristic of the church can be found throughout the writings of the earliest Christians.[3] The record of the patristic writers is clear and strong: there is only one church, scattered throughout the earth. The early church embraced, taught, and lived out the truth of the church's catholicity by staying focused on the essential mission given to them by Jesus, not by majoring on their idiosyncrasies or differences.

Sadly, in the centuries that have passed, we have departed from this emphasis on catholicity. Our lack of unity may well be the greatest weakness in the church today, and it is certainly not a strength to be exploited. The modern church seems smugly satisfied with its individualistic, antihistorical understanding of the Christian faith. But this is a far cry from the faith of the early followers of Christ.

When faithful pastors and church leaders begin to grasp this truth and then preach it to their congregations, I guarantee you will see something new happen. All hell breaks loose when we begin to emphasize the unity and catholicity of God's people. And I mean this literally! I am convinced that Satan hates a unified church and will do his best to oppose all who work and pray for unity. He will use aggressive tactics, defame our character, and subject us to vicious gossip—whatever he can do to discourage and dissuade us from following Christ in mission with other Christians. Wonderful Christian people will not understand our passion for working with others, at least initially. Many people have lived with these divisions for so long that they have no ability to see or understand why unity really matters.

Many years ago, someone taught me a simple and important principle: If the Holy Spirit teaches you anything, he will also call you to live it out. Those who recognize God's desire for unity and begin to obey his commands will also need to learn how to forgive others, since every effort at unity involves misunderstandings among sinful people. You are guaranteed to get hurt! We simply cannot undertake this kind of praying and teaching without the Holy Spirit's grace and power. Thank God that he gives what we need, each day, as we depend on him to lead and direct our efforts and to keep us watchful and aware of the enemies at work in our midst. We will need a growing awareness of the causes of disunity in order to move past the divisive spirit that has characterized the church for far too long.

QUESTIONS FOR
DISCUSSION AND REFLECTION

1. How can the Apostles' Creed help us establish a solid basis for doctrinal fidelity that will allow Christians and churches to agree on core orthodoxy and pursue meaningful relationships in truth? What do you see as weaknesses in this approach? What are its strengths?

2. What problems have you encountered when Christians try to unite in relational and cooperational contexts without a doctrinal foundation anchored in the early church?

3. What has the Spirit taught you about unity that requires your obedience and potential suffering?

chapter nine

The Cause of Our Disunity

Nothing will so avail to divide the church as love of power.
John Chrysostom

He cannot possess the robe of Christ who rends and divides the church of Christ.

Cyprian

THE HUMAN DESIRE FOR UNITY is profoundly rooted in our collective experience. Though our hunger for unity has been tragically distorted by sin, I am convinced that this desire for unity with other human beings is deeply rooted in the divine image. The earliest Christians not only had this hunger for unity; they confessed that God redeemed our desire for unity by restoring it through the work of Christ.

This restored desire for human unity openly challenges the narrowness of spirit that has soiled the church's character and reputation for centuries, even leading it to embrace schism as if it were a mark of the faithful church.[1] But separatism is not an inherent aspect of a vibrant Christian faith. It is foreign to Christ's will in both doctrine and spirit. While separations will certainly occur (cf. 1 Corinthians 11:19), they should be exceptional, regrettable, and always handled with extreme caution.

Christians have argued and opposed each other for centuries. At times, this has led Christians to persecute other Christians, even to the point of putting them to death. Sadly, some churches seem to believe their sole purpose is to oppose other churches. A spirit of separatism, left unchecked, can easily become a part of your church's DNA and become profoundly harmful to Christ's mission.

DID THE EARLY CHURCH EXPERIENCE UNITY?

The time between AD 60 and 160 has sometimes been called the "tunnel period" of church history—a transitional period between the time of the apostles and the century or more after they died. In Acts, we see that the early leaders of the church worked to preserve unity between AD 30 to 62—the generation following the death of Jesus. This infant church shared a common core of faith evidenced by five historical realities:

- the historical person of Jesus of Nazareth
- the *koinonia* (fellowship) we see in believers after Jesus' ascension
- the basic beliefs (*kerygma*) shared by all of Jesus' followers
- the events at the Jerusalem Council as recorded in Acts 15
- the relationship among the various missions and leaders we read about in Acts

But what about the generation that followed them? Did the postapostolic church maintain this same unity? The evidence is strong that the unity of the church was preserved during this period through a basic agreement about the meaning of Jesus' life, death, and resurrection—a core message preserved in the *kerygma* and evident in the **Didache**. While tensions and disagreements between leaders were real, the testimony of history shows that a common core of belief and practice kept the church together.

As a young Christian, I was taught that the church was divided and confused immediately after the generation of the apostles. But the historical evidence fails to support this idea. Cults often suggest this notion as they seek to promote "new" revelations. However, some evangelicals have also used it to argue against historical traditions.

In his master's thesis, Stephen Francis Staten concluded that there was unity in the subapostolic church from AD 62 until at least 150. He points to a "discernible unity of belief" from the time following Jesus' resurrection through Peter's first proclamation at Pentecost and the clarifications at the Jerusalem Council all the way through the declarations of Ignatius and Justin. The unity of belief primarily involved the person and work of Jesus but also the practice of baptism and the Eucharist. According to Staten, as Christians talked with others about these two experiences, they gained "a heartfelt appreciation for the Christian enterprise in other places." Also, "a process of learning from one another and their resources enabled them to more firmly understand their common faith." They began to see themselves as one gathering with the common objective of seeing that every level of society "had an opportunity to the same gospel and incorporation into the *ekklesia* community."[2]

We should remember that during this period there was no standard creed and no identifiable single bishop. (Though my Catholic friends will likely disagree, many Catholic biblical scholars admit that the picture I have painted is accurate.) We do know there were real differences of opinion during this period. Matters such as eschatology and the question of whether Jewish Christians could continue some of their ancestral practices created divergent viewpoints. But the church steadfastly refused to be divided. Though there was no single doctrinal system, there was a developing unity of common beliefs.

THE SEEDS OF DISUNITY BEGIN TO GROW

One of the first accounts we have of the infant church (Acts 6:1–7) reveals a struggle with disputes that threatened the unity of the Jerusalem congregation. The actions the church took to resolve the disagreement may seem odd, but they simply demonstrate that the apostolic leaders took seriously the threat of disunity.

A friend recently noted that in the letters of John we find exhortations to relentless, self-sacrificial love (1 John 1:8–11) alongside raging polemics against false teachers inside the church (2:19–23). Undeniably, a real tension exists as we seek to balance these truths. Yet, even given the reality of false teachers in their midst, the early church somehow kept catholicity and purity of doctrine together.

In addition to the problems the Jerusalem congregation faced, there were disputes with the Judaizers, a group of people who continually challenged the core message of the gospel. These disputes created bitter controversies, as evidenced by Paul's letter to the Galatians (see 1:7–9; 2:1–5.). Yet further schisms arose as the church began to address an even greater error, the looming threat of Gnosticism.

Both the later patristic and medieval periods of history reveal that schism eventually divided the church deeply. Disagreements between powerful churches and leading bishops became widespread. Even in the Middle Ages, where we find some positive evidence of external unity, the Eastern and Western churches formally divided in AD 1054. External forms of unity were sometimes enforced, but these divisions simply revealed a deeper problem, namely, resistance to the mission of Christ and the work of the Holy Spirit.

Later, when the church in the East faced a serious external conflict that led to wide-scale martyrdom, the Western church refused to offer aid to their Eastern brothers and sisters. Help from the West could have saved the lives of besieged Eastern Christians. To this day, this lack of help is a sad mark against the church in the West. Within a generation of this terrible struggle in the East, the Western church was torn apart by the Protestant Reformation. This movement challenged the Catholic Church to renew itself but resulted in a massive schism leading to errors on every side. Eventually, these schisms resulted in the birth of several major divisions within historic Protestantism, leading to an endless variety of new churches built around human personalities and doctrinal differences.

Today, millions of Christian congregations hold the same core doctrines while continuing to express distinctively different patterns of thought, government, and worship, not to mention different understandings about what each one believes to be truly essential. This sad story of disunity led G. W. Bromiley to draw this conclusion:

> Far from presenting a picture of unity to the world, the church seems almost to give a warning example of disunity,

the very strength of faith and conviction giving depth and bitterness to the "unhappy divisions." The church may have a consciousness of its unity. But it cannot ignore the stubborn fact of its disunity. And in face of this fact its confession of unity can only seem to be a hollow mockery to itself and especially to the world.[3]

So how do we explain the story of all our factions and schisms? If unity is stamped on the DNA of every Christian and every church, how have we succeeded in repressing it? Why does Christ's prayer go unanswered in our time? I am sure of one thing: Idealistic dreams of unity will not bring about unity itself. So how can we minimize our present disunity through a proper pursuit of Spirit-given relational unity? How can we work together to enlarge the vision of a unified church, especially when so many of the world's most passionate Christians believe the status quo is fine?

THE CHURCH IN THE WORLD

The church is the bride of Christ. Christ gave us a mission to fulfill during this two-thousand year period of betrothal (Matthew 28:19–20). We have also been called to live out the unity of the triune God. Christ is the center, and we are to press into him, but this is precisely the need we have not worked out in our relationships with one another.

Different communities of Christians do many things that fall into the category of human preferences. Diversity is not bad per se. We can expect that churches in many cultures and contexts will reflect widely different expressions of faith—and I believe it is one reason for the success of the gospel in so many diverse cultures. Unlike Islam, we do not seek to conform Christians and cultures to one narrow way of expressing our faith.

A comparison with the individual Christian experience can prove helpful. We know that each of us is called to follow Christ (1 Corinthians 1:2). We know that holiness is necessary, even though we remain sinners. Sin permeates all we do, much like a dark stain in a fabric. We cannot escape this, but we must fight it. The same pattern is true in every congregation. As Geoffrey Bromiley observes, "It is because there is no sinless perfection of the church that disunity arises in the community of Jesus Christ for all its awareness and confession of unity."[4] If anyone tells you their church is entirely pure, then run away as fast as possible. But please realize that sinful churches can pursue a better course and engage in a serious struggle to pursue unity, as difficult as the task may be.

Recognizing that sin causes our disunity should be easier than it often is. What will prove more difficult is making the serious effort needed to apply real solutions—solutions that do not seem clear to most of us. I am inclined to think that if we began to discover solutions, we would fear these even more than our present disunity. History has so jaded us and sin has so distorted our vision that many of us have simply given up on our quest for unity.

QUESTIONS FOR DISCUSSION AND REFLECTION

1. In what ways do you find that Christians desire unity but fail to pursue it?

2. How did the early church retain unity while it still grew in diversity? Do you think we can pursue self-sacrificial love and a strong polemic against false teachers at the same time? How?

3. If sin is the reason we give up on achieving unity, how does repentance restore it? Are there steps you can take in your own life to restore unity that has broken down between you and other people, or between your church and other churches?

chapter ten

Sectarianism: Our Enemy

Sectarianism is seeking unity in uniformity rather than unity in diversity and expecting other Christians to comply fully with my views before I can have genuine fellowship with them.

Rex Koivisto

IN AN EARLIER CHAPTER, we looked at how the earliest Christians confessed what they had been taught by Jesus and the apostles by using a short creed at their baptism and in public worship. This creed stated the basic truths that stood at the center of the Christian faith and eventually became a summary statement of classical Christianity. We have seen how this creed underscored the oneness of the church by connecting the existence of the church directly to the work of the Holy Spirit.

So what keeps the church from adopting this approach in the twenty-first century? How can we pursue catholicity when the church exists in a myriad of groups? How do we regain the "big church" perspective I am advocating?

To be fair, there are upstanding Christians who do not think these divisions are a problem. As you've seen, I am profoundly committed to advancing Christ's mission and kingdom in a way that pursues unity with all Christians. The reason for my passion is vividly illustrated by a prominent Protestant theologian in referring to the work of Christ in India. The leader of the "untouchables" in India renounced the caste system, and he urged his 60 million fellow untouchables to renounce the Hinduism that had been responsible for the caste system. But Christianity held no appeal as a possible alternative to Hinduism. "We are united in Hinduism," they said, "and we shall be divided in Christianity."[1] The argument was unanswerable.

THE PROBLEM: SECTARIANISM

I believe that the underlying problem in our quest for unity is sectarianism. Gaining a better understanding of this problem can help us begin to pursue unity together. The nineteenth-century theologian Philip Schaff expressed this clearly:

> Variety in unity and unity in variety is the law of God in nature, in history, and in his kingdom. Unity without variety is dead uniformity. There is beauty in variety. There is no harmony without many sounds, and a garden encloses all kinds of flowers. God has made no two nations, no two men or women, not even two trees or two flowers, alike. He has endowed every nation, every church, yea, every individual Christian with peculiar gifts and graces. His power, his wisdom, and his goodness are reflected in ten thousand forms.[2]

I do not believe that we have to give up our theological distinctions to pursue unity. In fact, any pursuit of unity that denies our uniqueness and diversity is not positive. Most people approach differences with others as a choice between right and wrong, as a zero-sum game with winners and losers. But I believe there is a better way — the pursuit of catholic diversity, a diversity that fosters vitality.

Catholic diversity is the opposite of sectarianism. *Sectarianism* derives from the Latin *secta* — "a path, a way, a method, a party or faction." The word implies mutual exclusivity, an exclusivity that thrives where people and groups believe they have a superior claim to truth. Sectarians believe their church/denomination/tradition can best "represent the body of Christ, to the exclusion or minimization of other genuinely Christian groups."[3]

I agree that everyone should believe that the church they embrace is the "right" one. Problems often arise, though, when Christians and churches believe that their brand of Christianity is *entirely* right — a way of thinking rooted in the notion that I am one who believes the truth and you believe a lie. It inflames our pride and promotes attitudes that oppose catholicity. We must resist the kind of intellectual certitude that will not allow for change and growth in one's own perspective and understanding. All truth can be viewed as truth, but from different perspectives. This is *not* postmodern relativism in any sense of the term.

Another way to think about this is to consider the problems faced in many countries in which tribal groups hinder national governments from functioning well. Tribalism can wreak havoc, breaking down families and communities and starting wars. Sectarianism is what we find when Christianity embraces a kind of social tribalism and lacks the willingness to engage with others who are different.

If you look up *sectarian* in your English dictionary, you will find synonyms such as *narrow-minded*, *parochial*, and *limited*. In the ancient church, *sectarian* described apostates who broke away from the catholic church. In the modern sense, I am using the term to express *exclusivity*. Multnomah Bible College professor Rex Koivisto states,

> The church must have a degree of diversity along with its unity. But sectarianism provokes diversity without the requisite New Testament relational unity. This kind of mutual exclusivity runs counter to the nature of the church itself. Such exclusiveness is a sectarianism of the worst sort. The Christian community envisioned in the New Testament is *one* church, a church catholic ... [and this requires] *a relational unity*. That is mandated. And that requires an end to *sectarian attitudes* [italics added].[4]

I defended sectarianism for decades. I instinctively knew in my heart that there were other Christians in other churches, but I had no place in my affections for Roman Catholics, the Orthodox, or even some (less conservative) Protestants. This is why the "conversion" moment I experienced was so life-changing for me.

I still describe myself with the terms *evangelical, Reformed, Protestant*—all used in a classical historical sense. But now I have developed deep friendships with Roman Catholics and the Orthodox, as well as numerous brands of Protestants. My sectarianism is not entirely gone, since I daily seem to find new ways of expressing religious pride. But I am beginning to realize just how much our pride and selfish conceit hinder the pursuit of Christian unity.

HOW INTELLECTUAL IDEOLOGY PRODUCES SECTARIANISM

When you become a Christian, you are not delivered from the mind-set of ideology, a mind-set that is deeply interested in abstract ideas and battles and possesses a magnetic appeal to people who engage in intellectual theology. The Catholic University of America professor Claes Ryn elaborates:

> The ideological mind-set, formed as it is at bottom by a desire to dominate rather than illuminate, is an intruder in philosophy and the arts. It is closed in on itself and resentful of competition. Instead of cultivating the openness to new influences that marks real philosophy [theology] and art [biblical storytelling] and letting itself be exposed to the possible intellectual turmoil of fresh insight, ideology shunts inconvenient thought and imagination aside. Ideologues produce propaganda, although sometimes propaganda of a sophisticated kind. When such individuals set the tone, the intellectual and artistic life suffers.[5]

True Christian knowledge is intrinsically humble. It re-actualizes biblical and historical truths by showing the inadequacy of strands of truth as an expression of the complete truth. A vital, dynamic Christian faith is not given or received through human theological systems. Theological systems can never be final because Christ, who is the truth, is the real object of faith. We believe in him and spend a lifetime seeking to understand what we believe. The truth of faith is actually found in the confessing act itself. The reason is eschatological. Until Christ returns, all our attempts to express the truth are severely limited by sin. Thus, all theological truth claims must remain biblically contestable so the church remains truly open to the Spirit.

This does not mean that all truth claims are relative or that Christian confession is nonbinding; it simply means that all human knowledge is ultimately provisional. We cannot put the beauty of revealed truth into human formulas. The future is the focal point of ultimate truth. All dogmatic statements are merely human hypotheses that should be tested for coherence with related knowledge.

Human systems of theology have a proper place in protecting and guiding the church. But when these systems become "the system of doctrine taught in the Holy Scriptures," we run into serious problems. I have heard conservative ministers argue that a historically conditioned statement of faith is *the* biblically correct system of true divinity. But Scripture is clearly not so much a treatise on systematic theology as the unfolding story of a people—the people of God. God gave us multiple stories that are woven into this one great story. But when we turn this macro-story into a "system of doctrine," we begin to live as if getting right doctrine is the same as living right. The result will very often be loveless Christians and churches who believe they control the truth.

A long and established Christian tradition argues that sin profoundly affects our ability to perceive truth. We may think we have unsullied access to the truth, but sin hinders our understanding. When we receive God's grace, do we resolve this problem of knowing and seeing? The answer lies in Hebrews 11, which tells us that we walk by faith and not by sight. A humble and faithful Christian life is marked by "fear and trembling" (Philippians 2:12) and a willingness to allow for **mystery**. Even John Calvin argued that "the knowledge of faith consists in assurance rather than in comprehension." He defined faith's knowing quality as a "solid constancy of persuasion" that results in "confidence."[6] By confidence, Calvin did not mean intellectual certitude but personal trust and assent, which "is more [about] the heart than the brain."[7]

The central problem is related to an error introduced by the philosopher René Descartes (1595–1650). Descartes believed that a deductive system of theology could be built on proofs like those discovered in mathematics. This approach created a category of thinking that severed faith and divine revelation from the self-attesting *Logos*, who is Jesus of Nazareth. In other words, if we are creatures, then our knowledge is necessarily built on analogy; it is derivative. We should never question the person of Christ, whom we came to know through divine revelation, but we should not adopt an attitude that suggests we know exactly what God knows.

The approach I advocate does not embrace illogical ways of thinking but allows us to see how faith transcends logical categories. To reject the modern category of certainty does not mean the only choice left is postmodern relativism. All claims to knowledge are useful so long as we understand them to be human pointers that help us know the one who is the final word.

The Christian theologian Lesslie Newbigin provides a brilliant historical overview of how we moved from understanding ultimate reality as personal knowledge—something gained in a relationship—to seeing it as impersonal knowledge of facts. "Personal knowledge is impossible without risk; it cannot begin without an act of trust, and trust can be betrayed. We are here facing a fundamental decision in which we have to risk everything we have. There are no insurance policies available"[8]

According to Newbigin, these types of thinking radically diverge in two ways. The first difference has to do with the issue of where our certainty rests. *For Christians, all certainty must rest in the person of Jesus Christ.* Newbigin writes,

> If the place where we look for ultimate truth is in a story and if (as is the case) we are still in the middle of the story, then it follows that we walk by faith and not by sight. If ultimate truth is sought in an idea, a formula, or a set of timeless laws or principles, then we do not have to recognize the possibility that something totally unexpected may happen.[9]

If our certainty rests on the faithfulness of Jesus Christ, whose gospel is revealed to us in his story, then we have to walk by faith, not by sight (or by system).

The second difference has to do with the fact that *there are two ways to understand seeing and hearing.* In the classical view, knowledge is *theoria*—"the vision of eternal truth," writes Newbigin. Based on seeing a truth, we can put it into action by *praxis*—"ways of embodying it in action."[10] In this approach, these two steps became the way we lived and confessed our faith. It is the way I was taught to preach and teach—a way I now realize is not found in Scripture. I was taught that a sermon went something like this: Tell them what the text says and then apply it to their lives.

In the biblical view, "ultimate reality is personal, ... faith comes by hearing, and unbelief is disobedience."[11] Unbelief is not just a failure to understand a deep puzzle solved by exegesis and philosophy. Dietrich Bonhoeffer got it right: "Only he who believes is obedient, and only he who is obedient believes."[12]

Many Christians seem to have inherited a deeply flawed view of ultimate reality and would benefit from rethinking how the human mind creates ideologies and uses a personal ideology as a way of knowing and describing God—which can cause us to be divided not so much by a particular doctrine as by the way we express a particular doctrine.

Christians who make ideology central will fight to preserve human systems and give up asking the greatest questions and engaging in honest exploration for the knowledge of God; instead, they will tend to confidently settle for answers rooted in powerful arguments or persuasive persons. If we are not careful, we give up serious reflection and cease to be sensitive to the complexity of divine truth. Theology can become a religious pursuit rather than a spiritual journey—a pursuit in which we might even idolize the human intellect and craft our own concepts of truth. The result is a virtual loss of the biblical tradition of wisdom. In this setting, knowledge is pursued not to draw our souls into the love of Christ but to get answers to questions posed by our ideology.

A friend helped me understand this through a simple equation: *knowledge + compassionate servanthood = wisdom*. When we adopt an ideological approach to Christianity, we travel a road that inevitably leads to sectarianism. And when we follow this road for a long time, a knock on the door of our souls may well demonstrate that no one is home. Our lives will have become filled with arguments, and our souls will be profoundly emptied of Christ's love.

BLESSED ARE THE PEACEMAKERS

As a result of sectarianism, I reduced the church to my own ideas. I utilized a personal checklist to determine who was in and out. When I came to realize this, I was filled with incredible remorse. Having spoken against many of God's servants, I was compelled by the Spirit to seek forgiveness and make restitution. I wrote personal letters to some leaders and asked them to forgive me for the way I had abused their reputation. Most graciously forgave me.

The sad part of my story is that when I openly confessed my pride, I became more vulnerable to sectarians who felt I had abandoned the truth. I confess I have not entirely recovered from this reaction. I try to respond properly to criticism from other Christians, but this remains a work in progress. In my flesh I still want to fight back. But God has shown me that this response is a denial of what I now believe about the church.

When I began moving away from sectarianism, I found remarkable peace. I no longer had to make my personal battles God's battles. I found I could pursue peace with other Christians in ways I never imagined. As I was wrestling with this upheaval in my life, the Lord drove me to the Scriptures and led me to meditate deeply on this text:

> Do not repay anyone evil for evil. Be careful to do what is right in the eyes of everyone. If it is possible, as far as it depends on you, live at peace with everyone. Do not take revenge my dear friends, but leave room for God's wrath, for it is written: "It is mine to avenge, I will repay," says the Lord. On the contrary:
>
> > "If your enemy is hungry, feed him;
> > if he is thirsty, give him something to drink.
> > In doing this, you will heap burning coals on his head."
> > Do not be overcome by evil, but overcome evil with good.
> > *Romans 12:17–21*

Eventually I learned that I had to surround myself with friends who could help me in my spiritual formation.[13] I needed to learn how to repay good for evil. When people asked me about a particular person or ministry, I tried to find a positive way to bless others. Another text helped me discover fresh grace: "Make every effort to live in peace with everyone and to be holy; without holiness no one will see the Lord" (Hebrews 12:14). I had to ask, "Was my effort to live in peace truly serious?"

In another context, but through words that transcend a specific context, Paul wrote, "Let us therefore make every effort to do what leads to peace and to mutual edification" (Romans 14:19). Was I willing to "make every effort" to seek peace?

But didn't Jesus say, "I did not come to bring peace, but a sword" (Matthew 10:34)? Though this saying of Jesus may seem contradictory to the Bible's call to peacemaking, the idea is that because of Jesus, there is conflict between the forces of darkness and light. Christians live in the light, and thus the darkness will hate them. Ministers are told to expose error and protect the church of Christ. I am convinced that faithful ministers must teach the truth and protect the church. But the question remains: How do we do this?

WHY CATHOLICITY MATTERS

One of the finest definitions for the word *catholic* is found in the writings of Cyril of Jerusalem (AD 348), who wrote shortly after the persecutions of the Roman emperors had come to an end.

> The church is thus called "catholic" because it is spread throughout the entire inhabited world, from one end to the other; and because it teaches in its totality [*katholikos*] and without leaving anything out every doctrine which people need to know relating to things both visible and invisible, whether in heaven or on earth. It is also called "catholic" because it brings to obedience every sort of person—whether rulers or their subjects, the educated and the unlearned. It also makes available a universal [*katholikos*] remedy and cure for every kind of sin.[14]

The church is to be found where the apostolic faith is found. According to Luke Timothy Johnson, to see the church as catholic (*katholikos*, "throughout the whole") means embracing both "a universality of extent and an inclusiveness that embraces differences within a larger reality and unity."[15]

I remain convinced that catholicity is where Christ's mission will be recovered in the present age. We may not live to see the complete healing of the tragic divisions in the Christian church—those that occurred in the eleventh century between the East and West and then those that came about in the sixteenth century in the West. At the same time, we must remind ourselves that nothing is impossible with God. We can embrace the apostolic framework seen in Scripture and take the first step toward embracing the truth of what Cyril stated so clearly. I believe this first step will change your life, as it did mine.

CATHOLICITY		
Growing Rigidity		*Growing Laxity*
Sectarianism	Denominationalism	Latitudinarianism
Authority only	Authority and liberty	Liberty only
Everything matters doctrinally	Some things matter doctrinally	Nothing matters doctrinally
Enlarged core of orthodoxy ⟵	Historic core of orthodoxy	⟶ Diminished core of orthodoxy
Narrow ground of fellowship	Broad ground of fellowship	No ground of fellowship
Tradition ignored and confused	Tradition recognized and used	Tradition disregarded

Figure 10.1: Taken from Rex Koivisto, *One Lord, One Faith* (2nd ed.; Eugene, Ore.: Wipf & Stock, 2009), 116. Used by permission of Wipf and Stock Publishers. *www.wipfandstock.com*.

QUESTIONS FOR DISCUSSION AND REFLECTION

1. In what ways do the divisions of the church hinder our work among those who are not yet Christians? Is this a growing problem in North America? How and why?

2. Where do you see sectarianism in your own life and church? What practical steps can you take to confront and overcome it?

3. What would happen if we truly made every effort to be at peace with all people? If you have experienced a local church schism, do you believe the participants in the debate were making every effort to pursue peace? Think of other examples of which you are aware.

4. How would you define *catholicity* if someone asked you to explain it? What does the term mean to you?

chapter eleven

Thinking Rightly about the Church

The church is present wherever "the manifestation of the Spirit" takes place.
Jürgen Moltmann

The church is the community founded by Jesus Christ and anointed by the Holy Spirit.
A Concise [Roman Catholic] Dictionary of Theology

SOME CHRISTIAN LEADERS meet the challenge of disunity with new proposals for a federation of churches; others believe the best answer is for everyone to join the *right* church. The problem with both of these solutions should be obvious to Christians who have been praying for and talking about unity for a long time. Some settle for a much smaller goal, namely, more personal fellowship among Christians and churches. Instinctively, we all know that something needs to change if the church is to accomplish its mission, but we are not sure where to begin. I suggest we begin by reflecting on a simple question: What is the church?

Twentieth-century ecumenical movements accomplished a great deal more than some realize. If nothing else, they led Christians to meet and pray with one another while they discussed subjects related to Christian faith and order. Meeting believers from other traditions, listening to them, and learning to love them are always good goals. It opens people up to the Holy Spirit's work in unique ways. I have shared how this has had a profound impact on my own life. Furthermore, these various expressions of ecumenism removed many barriers erected as a result of prejudice and ignorance.

But the twentieth-century ecumenical movement failed on several counts. For starters, the major points of doctrinal diversity that kept Catholic, Protestant, and Orthodox Christians separate still remain. Some communions sat out efforts to heal the schisms that have existed for centuries. The good news is that real differences can now be better handled with respect and patience while we still pursue new relationships.

THE "NEW ECUMENISM"

Much of the formal twentieth-century ecumenical movement got sidetracked when it began to embrace aspects of theological diversity that were not always faithful to Christ's mission. At times, this was fueled by socialist and liberationist ideologies. A significant loss to the movement was the absence of evangelicals and Roman Catholics—an absence being addressed in the twenty-first century by a "new ecumenism."[1]

Evangelicals have never completely abandoned the ecumenical process. This was evidenced by the birth of the Evangelical Alliance in 1846, when representatives of ten nations met in London to talk about unity and to work together on mission. The Evangelical Alliance was renamed World Evangelical Fellowship in 1951 and World Evangelical Alliance in 1982. WEA is "a global ministry working with local churches around the world to join in common concern to live and proclaim the Good News of Jesus in their communities." WEA's evangelical alliance of churches in 128 nations and over 100 international organizations have joined "to give a worldwide identity, voice, and platform to more than 420 million evangelical Christians. Seeking holiness, justice, and renewal at every level of society—individual, family, community, and culture—God is glorified, and the nations of the earth are forever transformed."[2]

One interesting and important development is a recent initiative called Christian Churches Together in the USA. CCT began in September 2001 with a meeting of church leaders who saw the need for expanding fellowship, unity, and witness among the diverse expressions of Christian faith. Lamenting the absence of a place where representatives of historic Protestant, Roman Catholic, Pentecostal, Evangelical, and Orthodox churches could strengthen their unity in Christ and empower their mission, the group convened another meeting in April 2002 to continue to explore and to invite broader participation from other church leaders.[3]

Much of this new ecumenism is happening in informal ways as the Holy Spirit draws various Christians together for prayer, community service, and mission. In this context we realize differences remain, much as they do in an extended family, but we are also discovering that we are in the same household of faith. (C. S. Lewis spoke of this household as a great mansion in which we all share the great hall while we each have rooms within the larger house.)

An interesting twist to all of this recent initiative for unity is the expanding postdenominational forms of Christianity that are the fastest-growing expressions of the church in the new century. The *World Christian Encyclopedia* estimates that roughly 20 percent of the world's 2.2 billion Christians are now part of what it calls "independent Christianity." These expressions are referred to as "forms of faith and worship separated from, uninterested in, and independent of historic, denominationalist Christianity."[4] The upside is that many of these believers and churches simply think of themselves as "Christians"; the downside is that sometimes there is far too little concern for the rest of the Christian family.

In America, various attempts at unity have failed among evangelicals for virtually the same reason they failed in liberal ecumenical settings—ideology has trumped mission. On both the right and the left we have been far more successful at partisan politics and social issues than at discovering our spiritual relationship in the mission of Christ. I have a simple thesis regarding why: It is much easier to unite around a social or political agenda than to work for the relational oneness of Christ's people in a vibrant missional context where we must work hard to break down barriers and build bridges.

MIXED FRUIT

Protestant denominations have an uncertain future. It now seems that unless they redefine themselves in terms of Christ's mission, they will come to very little over the next century. The danger now is different than in the past. Christians are increasingly forming new churches around sectarian impulses. At the very moment in history when the door to relational unity is opening, many churches may miss this unique opportunity to build relationships with other Christians. The result would be further division. I am not suggesting that all of the doctrinal points emphasized in these "new" churches are irrelevant. Some of their doctrinal concerns have the power to strengthen the church at large. But these new forms and perspectives are not the core of our common faith.

Churches all over the world are being formed around the gifts of the Spirit or around uniquely gifted leaders. Movement-based Christianity remains hugely attractive. How do we address what appears to be a genuine move of the Holy Spirit while we strive for relational unity?

Our disunity remains an incontestable fact. On one side we have older churches that disdain the "independent," postdenominational trends, while on the other we have a flush of excitement about these newer movements. The church of "what's happening now" often becomes the new church of the twenty-first century. I believe the solution is for Christians to first cultivate a love for catholicity and then prayerfully reach across our divisions, challenging each other to embrace the mission of Christ together.

WHAT IS THE CHURCH?

The mere mention of the word *church* sends some Christians into emotional apoplexy. They love Jesus, but the church is another matter. In some cases, people have been profoundly harmed by the church. In other cases, their experience of the church has been dull and unfulfilling. Still others have found the church to be a religious corporation that seems completely irrelevant. I am sympathetic toward these reactions, but the truth is this: A simple reading of the Bible will convince us that a person cannot be a serious and faithful Christian without being vitally related to the church. And being united with the people of God will mean we will be in relationships with flawed people.

We all identify ourselves by naming the people and events that have shaped us. Christians are no different. We are identified by the people we associate with. But Christians are also members of God's community. We may wish to downplay this family relationship, but our salvation is never solitary. We are saved as the people of God called to live in community. There are two traps to be avoided here—(1) pseudo-pious *sentimentality* in which we fail to see that the church must have organization and (2) *institutionalism* in which we fail to see that the church is a living organism.

We are not saved to live a solitary life. Eugene Peterson captures this well: "God never makes private, secret salvation deals with people. His relationships with us are personal, true; intimate, yes; but private, no. We are a family in Christ. When we become Christians, we are among brothers and sisters in faith. No Christian is an only child."[5]

The New Testament presents a lovely portrait of the church by using different terms to describe our identity. These terms clearly overlap and allow us to see the rich tapestry of our oneness as a global community.

ONE COMMUNITY, DIFFERENT TERMS

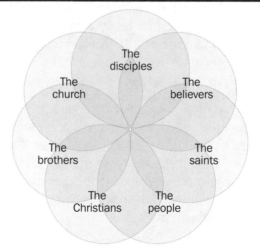

Figure 11.1: Taken from *The Dictionary of the Later New Testament and Its Development*, edited by Ralph P. Martin and Peter H. Davids. Copyright © 1997 by InterVarsity Christian Fellowship/USA. Used by permission of InterVarsity Press, PO Box 1400, Downers Grove, IL 60515. *www.ivpress.com*.

This biblical portrait underscores the point that true Christianity involves human relationships because all of life, as the Jewish philosopher Martin Buber suggested, is "encounter." This idea stretches back to the covenant of creation through the Abrahamic covenant, Sinaitic covenant, and Davidic covenant to the new covenant established through the sacrifice of Jesus. Salvation is never an individual matter. At Pentecost, the Holy Spirit was poured out on all who were gathered—an outpouring without respect of ethnicity, race, or gender. The book of Acts provides a marvelous account of the historical development of this truth.

But what is the church? Many people answer by providing a list of things the church does or by describing things that are *not* the church (for example, it is not a building or a legal organization or society). In its most simple form, *church* describes "the people of God." The New Testament Greek word for *church* refers to "an assembly or congregation that has been called out for a specific purpose." What makes the New Testament church distinctive is that it belongs to Jesus Christ. It is called by him for his purpose.

The English word *church* comes from the Old English *cirice* (ultimately from the Greek *kyriakos*, "of the Lord"). Thus the building where people met was sometimes called "the Lord's house," not in the sense that God dwelled only there, but in the sense that "the Lord's people" met there.

I do not advocate giving up the word *church*. But we desperately need to reform our understanding. Some popular evangelical writers dehistoricize the church and make a case for revolution, not reformation. They throw out the past. The theology behind this idea is deficient, and the approach has been tried many times in history, with less than positive results. Generally, this approach results in new schism and radical sectarianism. It has led some to assert that they have recovered the *true* church since they have followed the biblical blueprint. Because of the various claims that groups make about the church, we must seek to understand the word much better. I conclude that the church is *the people of God*, and as his people we will always need spiritual renewal.

The early Protestant Reformers rightly believed that where the Word of God is preached and the sacraments administered, a real gathering of the church happens. (Some added discipline as a third mark.) I would add two biblical marks: mission and a deep commitment to justice and the poor. These two additional marks are consistently seen in the prophetic writings, in the life and ministry of Jesus, and in the life and practice of the earliest Christians.

The late Reformed theologian John Leith wrote, "The church exists where the Word of God is heard in faith and obeyed in love."[6] Nothing else is really necessary for the church to exist in space and time. Ignatius (AD 110) stated, "Wherever Jesus Christ is, there is the catholic church" — a concise statement, written long before the church took on profound external structure. The church is the people of God hearing, believing, and obeying the Word of God. I suggest that this understanding is inherent to the New Testament story. More can be said, but this generous and faithful definition promotes relational unity without compromising important differences.

THE CHURCH UNDERSTOOD AS THE LOCAL CONGREGATION

Within the New Testament, the term *church* is most often applied to Christians who gather in a specific place. The church is a local congregation in a particular place. This church could be seen because it consisted of real people in real human relationships. Paul's letters address specific problems in congregations. It is here, week after week, that we confess our Christian faith, receive baptism, come to the Lord's Table, and worship God with our fellow believers.

So strong is this biblical emphasis that some Christians have insisted that it is the only correct use of the word *church*. The problem is that the New Testament shows that no congregation ever existed apart from other congregations. Simply stated, the congregation is the church. One local congregation is as much the church as any other church. But the church is also the whole of all such congregations throughout the whole earth. So the church is both the local congregation and the whole people of God. (This universal emphasis on the church is particularly clear and strong in Paul's letter to the Ephesians.) My friend Craig Higgins correctly observes that being *the church* and being a part of *a church* are really two sides of the same coin! He adds that there are no "Christians at large."[7]

THE CHURCH IN THE CITY

The church is also addressed in the New Testament as existing in one city or region, such as the church in Jerusalem, Antioch, Rome, or Ephesus. As I read the New Testament, I see three dimensions of the church. The most frequent use is with reference to a local congregation that meets in a specific place (often a single house church). The second use is that of the universal church, or all those who believe. But a third dimension offers incredible practical possibilities. The church was the collection of all the house churches in one city, such as in Rome, where several such gatherings are referenced (cf. Romans 16:3–5, 14–15). It seems evident that a simple reading of the text will lead one to conclude that *local church* had two meanings: (1) a single congregation gathering in a certain place (a home or later a building) and (2) a group of congregations in a particular city that may have met together on occasion but likely met as different congregations most of the time.

Rex Koivisto diagrams this point clearly.

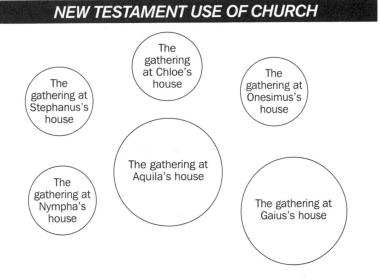

Figure 11.2: Taken from Rex Koivisto, *One Lord, One Faith* (2nd ed.; Eugene, Ore.: Wipf & Stock, 2009), 10. Used by permission of Wipf and Stock Publishers. *www.wipfandstock.com.*

When a congregation sees itself as "the church" in a given location to the exclusion of other congregations that meet in the same location, it breeds isolation and sectarianism. Sadly, this seems to be the present state of most churches in America. The strong emphasis of most congregations is on their own ministry to the exclusion of that of other local churches. While it is right to acknowledge the universality of the church, it seems equally right that we recover the biblical emphasis on all the congregations in our particular community. Rex Koivisto convinced me that this way of thinking can bear incredible fruit if Christian leaders begin to lead their congregations (and ministries) to think of themselves as part of a larger whole. Here is how Koivisto demonstrates what this point might look like in his own city of Portland, Oregon. (This graph is *not* inclusive enough, but the point is clearly made!)

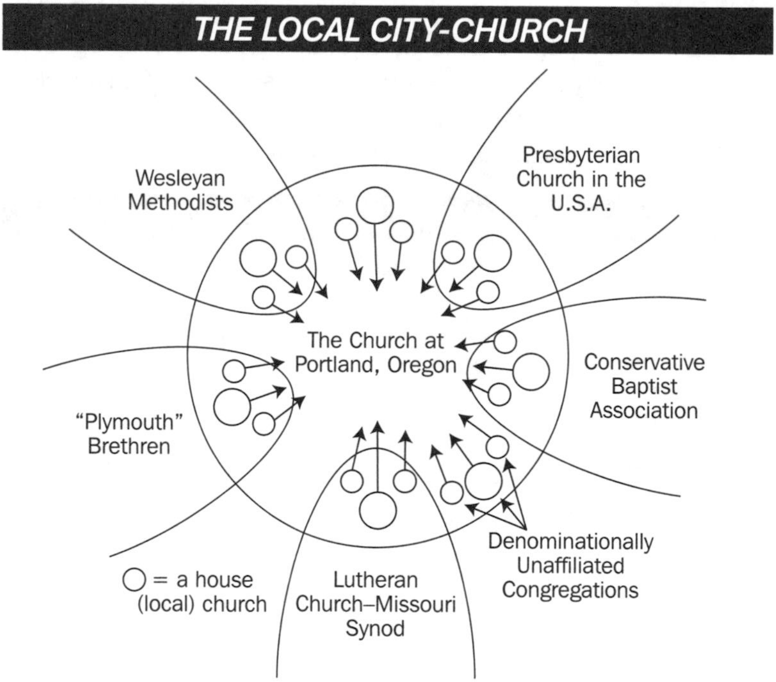

THE LOCAL CITY-CHURCH

Figure 11.3: Taken from Rex Koivisto, *One Lord, One Faith* (2nd ed.; Eugene, Ore.: Wipf & Stock, 2009), 120. Used by permission of Wipf and Stock Publishers. *www.wipfandstock.com.*

As the church developed during the fourth and fifth centuries, it grew increasingly close to the state, leading to a system whereby each town had one church—the "parish" church. In modern society, especially in an increasingly post-Christian American context, this concept is dead. Our task is not to form parishes but to be the people of God in a mixed society where we live among those who are not yet in the church. We are to be the church for *them*, not for us. We are to live so they will find the grace of God among us. We do this best when we begin to recognize the one church in our city. This concept would radically alter the ministry of almost every congregation I know if it were put into practice by the leaders. I will demonstrate in chapter 18 how some leaders are pursuing this concept in practice, with a growing vision of city transformation.

THE CHURCH – UNIVERSAL, LOCAL, INVISIBLE, VISIBLE

It seems quite evident that early Christian believers confessed faith in a church that covered the earth. The universality of this church was important because it kept them from limiting the church to one nationality, class of people, or race. Without this understanding we can easily move away from mission into a protective institutional organization that can become racist, nationalistic, or misogynistic.[8]

It is important to recognize that the church is not the sum of the total number of local congregations added together to form one worldwide church made up of thousands of smaller parts. In reality, every single church is a true church in its own place, and at the same time every church is the church catholic. Catholicity is a *quality*, not an *organization*. It is a spiritual quality that belongs to every church. The total body of believers can only be found in the universal church, yet a single congregation has every right to call itself a church because it shares in the life and mission of Jesus.

The church is both visible and invisible. Since the church is a spiritual reality it must be invisible in one sense. But as we saw earlier, this use of the word *spiritual* doesn't mean "opposed to the physical/material." As a spiritual totality, the catholic church is not found in one place or in one fellowship. Thus we can rightly say that the church, as the whole people of God, is invisible to our eyes. This is true with regard to both the church in heaven and the whole church on earth, at least in the sense that Paul put it in 2 Timothy 2:19 when he writes, "The Lord knows those who are his."

An old Scottish confession of faith captures the proper balance:

> The catholic or universal church, which is invisible, consists of the whole number of the elect that have been, are, or shall be gathered into one, under Christ the head thereof; and is the spouse, the body, the fullness of him that fills all in all.
>
> The visible church, which is also catholic or universal ..., consists of all those throughout the world that profess the true religion, together with their children; and is the kingdom of the Lord Jesus Christ, the house and family of God, out of which there is no ordinary possibility of salvation.[9]

The great value of this thinking is clear. The catholic church can only be visible at one moment and place. "We who are alive in Christ represent in one place and time that whole which God alone sees in its completeness. The great procession of the faithful crosses the world's stage—and only such part of it as is actually crossing the stage is visible; and as it passes through the world, [it is] a 'mixed multitude.' "[10]

A right understanding of invisibility reminds us that the unity of the church is ultimately God's work. But we can become captive to a deficient understanding if we no longer struggle with the way God actually works to bring about our relational unity. The visible church must be our primary concern since we are members together, and this church belongs to Jesus Christ.

QUESTIONS FOR DISCUSSION AND REFLECTION

1. How did twentieth-century efforts toward unity in the church succeed? How did they fail? Why do you think so much of the ecumenical movement failed to accomplish the goal of unifying the church? Should we engage in formal expressions of ecumenism? Why or why not?

2. How would you define *the church*? Is a local congregation the church? How does the idea of "the people of God" help you in your thinking about the church?

3. For the Protestant Reformers, what was necessary in order for there to be a church?

4. Is the church visible or invisible? In what sense is it one, the other, or both?

chapter twelve

The Servant Church and the Kingdom

The term "kingdom of God" might be more accurately translated "the reigning of God," affirming that the kingdom is the Lord's.

Christian Word Book

The kingdom of heaven is continually growing and advancing to the end of the world.

John Calvin

IMPORTANT WORDS JUMP OFF THE PAGES of Scripture when we read carefully. One such magnificent word is *kingdom*. The Protestant Reformers saw this word as vital to understanding the role of the church. Historically, Catholics equated the kingdom with the church. Many Catholic scholars believe this way of thinking significantly changed at Vatican II.

Biblical scholars agree that the *kingdom of God*, the *kingdom of Christ*, and the *kingdom of heaven* are synonymous. The idea of the kingdom is deeply rooted in the Old Testament and considerably developed in the New. Properly understanding the kingdom will go a long way toward helping us avoid a church that is too small.

THE REFORMATION AND EVANGELICAL UNDERSTANDING

In the Western understanding of the gospel, Jesus died for our sins, rose for our justification, and ascended to heaven to intercede for us. At the end of this age he will come again. The church was commissioned to spread this good news. Mission primarily referred to telling people that Jesus was crucified and raised for their salvation—an emphasis that was recovered in the Reformation.

As a child I sang, "I love to tell the story! 'Twill be my theme in glory—to tell the old, old story of Jesus and his love." I understood that the "old, old story" was about Jesus dying for me. I was taught that Scripture could be understood through three great realities—creation, fall, and redemption—sometimes reduced to a simple outline. All of this had a profound impact on my understanding of the church.

This type of thinking is not wrong; it just doesn't go far enough. Combined with Western individualism, this stress on personal salvation misses the narrative (story line) of the Bible and gives people another reason not to care deeply about the church. The biggest problem with the Western emphasis is that it misses the cosmic dimensions of the gospel—"the universal nature of God's work in all of history."[1] A richer account of redemption follows the biblical themes of creation, incarnation, and re-creation. I believe this story line flows out of the reality of the kingdom of God. The words *creation*, *incarnation*, and *re-creation* "constitute a connecting symbol for the whole story of God."[2]

WHY JESUS BECAME FLESH

Jesus' primary purpose for coming into the world was not to save us and then take us to heaven; his central mission was to manifest the reign of God over all of creation. The proper understanding of his incarnation and atonement can be seen when Paul writes, "God was reconciling the world to himself in Christ" (2 Corinthians 5:19).

The kingdom of God is the central idea in God's cosmic redemption. George E. Ladd concludes that "there is no tension between 'the power and the kingdom of our God and the authority of his Christ' (Revelation 12:10)" because the terms are used in the exact same context.[3] Jesus said the kingdom of God was near (Mark 1:15), that people were called to conversion and repentance (Matthew 11:20–24; Luke 10:13–15; 13:1–5; 19:41–44), and that we should be ready and alert for the coming of the kingdom in the last day (Matthew 25:1–13; Luke 12:35–40).

Jesus' kingdom is not like any earthly kingdom. "My kingdom is not of this world," he said (John 18:36). Jesus did not mean that his rule was only spiritual but that it was not derived from earthly authorities. Paul adds that Christ will exercise this rule until he has put everything under the Father's reign (cf. 1 Corinthians 15:24–28). In Revelation 12:10, the kingdom of God is parallel with salvation, thus the kingdom is directly related to Christ's authority in the world. This includes much more than our personal salvation.

WHERE DO WE FIND THE KINGDOM?

In the broadest sense, the kingdom of God exists wherever God's will is at work—primarily where you find redeemed people serving Christ. The church thus manifests itself as a servant community to the kingdom. The New Testament sees two kingdoms at work in this world—one evil and one good. The redemptive rule of Christ has defeated the kingdom of Satan through his cross, and thus the results of Christ's victory are clear. If we understand this story, we see that we live between two great redemptive events—the first and second coming of Christ.

University of Notre Dame theology professor Richard McBrien writes, "Because there is no limit to the presence of God, the kingdom of God has no boundaries.... The kingdom of God is as broad and as overarching as the presence of God which renews and transforms and re-creates everything touched by it."[4] The kingdom of God existed before Christ came and becomes most clearly present in the person of Christ. He is revealed as the *Servant-Messiah*. The church thus exists as an outcrop of the kingdom and is a servant community that advances his kingdom.

THE THREE TENSES OF THE KINGDOM

The church's role is to announce the good news of the kingdom and demonstrate the reality of Christ's reign. Notice the three tenses involved in carrying out this role.

First, the kingdom has a *past tense*. The church proclaims that Jesus Christ has come. In Jesus' life, death, resurrection, and ascension, God invaded human history. Robert Webber writes, "God literally becomes his creation."[5] (Read that several times.) God is united with creation in Jesus Christ, and the redemption of the world is brought about by this man. The church gathers to celebrate this in Word and sacrament.

This kingdom also has a *present tense*. The church is a vibrant living sign of Christ's kingdom. We live as servants so that the presence of God is a healing, reconciling presence that seeks justice, peace, and true freedom. The church becomes an instrument through which God achieves the unity of the new creation. Here the cosmic story gains its hearing in this age. We proclaim that there is one person who is the solution—Jesus!

Finally, the kingdom includes a *future tense*. The church is here to show the world what lies ahead when Jesus Christ comes again. This is the re-creation part of the narrative. People need hope, and the biblical story gives it in abundance.

Christians debate the steps God will take to bring about the final phase of Christ's kingdom, but they all agree on the final goal—the consummation of human history in total re-creation. When the kingdom fully comes, God "will wipe away every tear from their eyes. There will be no more death or mourning or crying or pain, for the old order of things has passed away" (Revelation 21:4).

VATICAN II: CATHOLICS DISCOVER THE KINGDOM

Prior to Vatican II, many Catholics saw the parables of Jesus as synonymous with the church. Cardinal Walter Kasper rejects this idea: "The church is only an effective and accomplished sacramental sign, *not the reality of the kingdom of God itself*" (italics added).[6] Some Roman Catholics disagree with Cardinal Kasper and look with suspicion at anything outside the Catholic Church.

The Catholic conflation of the church with the kingdom was clearly a reaction to Protestant interpretation. A Catholic archbishop notes that this view led some to conclude that "the ultimate fulfillment of the kingdom will come when all have converted to Catholicism."[7] But Vatican II opened a new door of Catholic understanding about the kingdom.

George E. Ladd makes this accurate conclusion:

> The kingdom of God is *not* the church. The apostles went about preaching the kingdom of God (Acts 8:12; 19:8; 28:23); it is impossible to substitute "church" for "kingdom" in such passages. *However there is an inseparable relationship*. The church is the fellowship of the people who have accepted God's offer of the kingdom, submitted to its rule, and entered into its blessings.... The offer of the kingdom was made on an individual basis in terms of personal acceptance (Mark 3:31–35; Matthew 10:35–37) rather than in terms of family or nation [italics added].[8]

God saves individuals for the kingdom, but the kingdom is not primarily about the community. We can say the kingdom *creates* the community, which is the church. Both the rule of Christ and his redemptive work bring into being a new people who receive blessings through grace alone. This new community is the catholic church.

Catholic theologians who adopt this view could help pave the way toward opening a door for new relationships. Joseph Cardinal Ratzinger (Pope Benedict XVI) wrote about this in 1960. He appealed to the biblical basis for cooperation and argued that love can be perfected through God's fatherhood, Christ's divine sonship, and our brotherhood. Ratzinger wrote of two communities — Protestant and Catholic (and everything he says applies to the Orthodox as well). He admits we are not yet in the one visible mystery of the same church, which he believes to be the Roman Catholic Church. But he explains how our two communities can now receive each other as sister communities, treating individual Christians as "brothers to each other."[9] He concludes:

> Admittedly, this brotherhood between Catholics and Protestants includes the fact that both belong to a different

fraternal community—includes, too, the separation, and the pain of this separation, and thus presents a constant challenge to overcome it. Indeed, it is important not to ignore the element of separation which is inevitably part of this brotherhood and gives it its particular quality; to ignore it is ultimately to become reconciled to it, and that is just what we must not do.[10]

These insights may seem unimportant to Protestant readers. Our danger lies in the idolatry of concepts. We easily confuse the finite with the infinite, thus equating our experience of the church with the kingdom of God. For Protestants, the danger is found not in directly equating the kingdom with the church but in equating exegetical correctness with the kingdom.

THE IMPORTANCE OF *UNITATIS REDINTEGRATIO* (RESTORATION OF UNITY)

Vatican II, in the Decree on Ecumenism, calls "all the Catholic faithful to recognize the signs of the times and to participate skillfully in the work of ecumenism." This council laid out the steps that have allowed Catholics to "participate skillfully" in the Christian pursuit of unity. The document on ecumenism, titled *Unitatis Redintegratio*, has been crucial in the quest to correct common misunderstandings about the kingdom.

A fundamental concern at Vatican Council II was the restoration of unity among all Christians. The bishops believed the Holy Spirit dwelled in all Christians and was moving them toward the great goal of confessing the one faith. To this end, the document on ecumenism gave Catholics clear principles to follow in seeking unity. The statement reads, "This change of heart and holiness of life, along with public and private prayer for the unity of Christians, should be regarded as the soul of the whole ecumenical movement."[11] The decree urges Catholics to admit their faults with regard to breaking this unity. Recognizing constraints on worship, the document notes two principles governing common worship—the bearing of witness to the unity of the church and the sharing in the means of grace—and states, "Witness to the unity of the church very generally forbids common worship to Christians, but the grace to

be had from it sometimes commends this practice."[12] This underscores what has really happened over the last forty-five-plus years.
We still do not share common worship (sacramentally), but grace
commends it.

The council also declared that theology must be taught from
an ecumenical viewpoint. Catholic scholar John W. O'Malley
writes, "Some teachings ... are more fundamental than others, as, for instance, are those in the ancient creedal statements of the church.... Cooperation among Christians vividly
expresses the bond that already exists among them and sets
in clear relief the features of Christ the Servant, their master
and ideal."[13] Many Catholic biblical scholars have seen what
the Holy Scriptures make plain, namely, that the church "is the
whole body of Christians" and that the kingdom is served by
the church.[14]

These principles seem reasonable, but when they were written, they signaled a major shift. Earlier the council has said
that other Christian communities should "return" to the Catholic
Church. Later statements have suggested much the same, but
many Catholics believe there is an element of tension between
the council's dogma about the church and its expressed desire
for unity with non-Catholics. I believe the stronger voice, the one
expressing desire for unity, will ultimately win.

In a 1998 essay, Joseph Cardinal Ratzinger (Pope Benedict XVI) wrote, "Only when the person is struck and opened
up by Christ in his inmost depth can the other also be inwardly
touched, ... can true community grow." We sense something of
his heart when he writes of those who spoke of "winter in the
church" in the 1970s. "But suddenly here was something that
no one had planned. Here the Holy Spirit himself had, so to
speak, taken the floor.... Every irruption of the Holy Spirit always
upsets human plans."[15] He goes on to say this ever-renewing
work of the Spirit was going on within the basic structures of
the church. He saw awakenings of the Holy Spirit pushing the
church to discover unity in ways that sought reconciliation. This
thinking appears cautious (at least to me), but it plainly reveals
that Vatican II ecumenism is rooted in the ever-present ministry
of the Holy Spirit.

THE CHURCH AND THE KINGDOM RIGHTLY UNDERSTOOD

All Christians are called to bring about the kingdom of God in every aspect of life — church, family, work, community. Why? God's claim is over *all* of life — personal and communal, public and private, individual and collective. But this goes directly against the thinking of most North American Christians. We have been taught that all of life fits into one of two categories — secular or sacred. This dualistic hangover must be resisted on the basis of the biblical narrative, which clearly says that *all* of creation is good. The spheres of education, politics, and the marketplace all belong to Christ.

The church must engage the world afresh with the story of Jesus. This incredible news declares that everyone who trusts in Jesus will be saved. But it includes the servant work of God's people seeking to remove oppression, poverty, disease, and injustice. We will never transform the world entirely until Jesus comes. But we must bring Jesus to the whole world. Abraham Kuyper expressed this powerfully: "No single piece of our mental world is to be hermetically sealed off from the rest, and there is not a square inch in the whole domain of our human existence over which Christ, who is sovereign over *all*, does not cry: 'Mine!' "[16]

Karl Barth said the church was a "provisional representation" of the unity of all mankind, which was lost by the fall.[17] This restoration to unity happens when the redeemed are united in the one Christ who is Lord of all (see Ephesians 4:3–6).

RENEWAL IS STILL POSSIBLE

My observations lead me to conclude that the church *can* be corrected and renewed. The church is never above criticism. If it cannot be corrected, it is too small. Both Catholics and Protestants recognize this principle, though Protestants have been more open to it historically. The more we pursue church renewal, the better it is for the kingdom of God. I have also come to see that the primary mission of the church is not just to bring people into the visible church but to bring people into the knowledge of Christ and his kingdom.

I am convinced that humanity is starving for the unity God offers us in his kingdom. People have looked to secular humanism, Marxism, socialism, and capitalism to bring about unity. The only way we will ever experience the satisfaction of this divine hunger is to "see" and "enter" the kingdom of God (cf. John 3:3, 5) and then share this kingdom life in the fellowship of the local and global church.

QUESTIONS FOR DISCUSSION AND REFLECTION

1. How does a strong emphasis on the gospel as Christ's payment for our sins keep us from a balanced view that broadens our understanding of the church? Why did Jesus become human flesh?

2. What and where is the kingdom of God? What relationship does the church have to this kingdom? What do the three tenses of the kingdom mean?

3. How did Roman Catholics discover the kingdom teaching in Scripture? What difference does this make for real ecumenism today? What unique contribution did Pope Benedict XVI make to this thinking?

chapter thirteen

What Place Should We Give to Tradition?

The history of Christian doctrine is the most effective means available of exposing the artificial theories of continuity that have assumed normative status in the church, and at the same time it is an avenue into the authentic continuity of Christian believing, teaching, and confessing. Tradition is the living faith of the dead; traditionalism is the dead faith of the living.

Jaroslav Pelikan

The question is really not "Do I believe in tradition?" but, "Which tradition will I follow?" Every evangelical subculture is laden with traditions peculiar to its own history.

Robert E. Webber

THE WORD *TRADITION* has several connotations. For Catholic and Orthodox Christians, these connotations are mainly positive; for many evangelical Protestants, they are mainly negative. I am persuaded that unless we restore serious respect for Christian tradition, we are doomed to repeat the myriad of mistakes we have made with regard to unity and mission.

The *New Oxford American Dictionary* (2001) defines *tradition* as "the transmission of customs or beliefs from generation to generation." From the Latin *traditio* we get much closer to the biblical meaning of tradition: "handed over." The Greek word for *tradition* is *paradosis*, which refers to a truth transmitted or handed over.

Christian tradition has been handed over in written form — experienced directly in the Holy Scriptures. For Christians, Scripture acts as *the* norm. For Protestants, Scripture has been called "the *norming* norm." Tradition has also been handed down in oral form. Paul speaks of both forms when he writes, "So then, brothers and sisters, stand firm and hold fast to the teachings [traditions] we passed on to you, whether by word of mouth or by letter" (2 Thessalonians 2:15).

In the first several centuries of Christianity, there is no doubt that Christianity was passed on primarily through oral tradition. (The rabbinic law was passed along in the same manner and later written down; thus there was a precedent.) This oral tradition eventually took shape in written forms, principally in the Scriptures.

In historical usage, the term *tradition* has had a wide range of meanings. Early church scholar R. P. C. Hanson observes that "[tradition] can stand for the whole of Christianity as a complex of doctrines, practices, norms of behavior, cult and religious experience, handed down from the beginning."[1] While *tradition* has been popularly used to describe various types of post-canonical traditions such as the "Lutheran tradition" or the "Anglican tradition," Hanson identifies the heart of its meaning:

> Its proper and most widely accepted meaning is the teaching and practice of the church, formally distinct from the words of Scripture, as this teaching and practice has been carried on continuously from the beginning. In this sense tradition is a necessary part of historical Christianity, and no Christian denomination or communion has existed, or could have existed, without tradition, because all have taught and lived the Christian faith. Even those who have attempted to exist without tradition have only succeeded in establishing a tradition of dispensing with tradition.[2]

Many evangelicals oppose Christian tradition because they pit the spiritual against the historical. This is a false antithesis. Those who dispense with tradition always create new traditions. I believe many evangelicals are becoming weary of trendy Christianity. They know there has to be something more than the "newest" thing.

A negative response to Christian tradition often results in sectarianism. A growing number of younger evangelicals are discovering what the late Robert Webber called "ancient/future faith." They ask how this ancient faith, with all its rich tradition, can guide us toward a stronger future when the winds of secularism, modernism, and postmodernism are blowing with hurricane force against the church. They know that stronger ballast is needed. They are open to the idea that Christian tradition helps.[3]

CHRISTIAN TRADITION

Let's take a brief look at four components of Christian tradition.

BIBLICAL TRADITION

In the New Testament, there are two types of tradition: (1) the "human traditions," which are strongly condemned by Jesus in Mark 7:6–8, and (2) the holy or apostolic tradition, referred to by Paul, who tells us "to hold fast to the teachings [traditions] we passed on to you" (2 Thessalonians 2:15).

Tradition's importance pervades our lives on a daily basis. There are recognizable practices we all follow in family life, personal habits, work, government, and education. We choose to do this and not that. Why? The answers are often rooted in tradition. Without tradition, we do not function well.

Take science, for example. No one seriously works in science without embracing tradition. A new scientific investigator joins a community in which a body of accepted knowledge (tradition) has been present for hundreds of years. This tradition is open to all. There are right and wrong ways to do serious research. Even the best "original" thinkers build on the past. What is already there is scientific tradition. In the early church, we encounter virtually the same concept.

TRADITION IN CLASSICAL CHRISTIANITY

Each of the three great expressions of classical Christianity (Roman Catholic, Orthodox, Protestant) relies on tradition. One of the obvious ways they differ has to do with how they use and interpret tradition. If you become involved in serious ecumenism, you will soon discover this difference and its importance.

One thing is certain: *Tradition is important to all Christian faith and practice.* The earliest Reformers never jettisoned tradition. In fact, the Protestant Reformers developed arguments that profoundly respected the creeds and the ancient tradition. They argued that the papacy had abused Christian tradition by adding doctrines that were neither biblical nor found in the ecumenical creeds.

The Reformers argued that final authority was found in the Scripture, but they lived in profound historical continuity with the apostles, prophets, and early church fathers. The Hungarian Reformed theologian Béla Vassady writes, "The terms *evangelical* and *Reformed* should never have been used in contradistinction to each other. Nor should they ever have been employed to indicate confessional or denominational characteristics. They both represent basic, dynamic principles and for that reason are correlative with the term *catholic*."[4]

The Protestant Reformers believed in a "rule of faith" (summary) that was taught by all Christians everywhere. They believed that oral traditions began to end in terms of their normative importance around AD 300. They believed that new traditions were unable to withstand the written tradition of the New Testament. The church fathers agreed that early Christian tradition was identical with what Scripture taught. Writers such as Irenaeus and Tertullian regularly appealed to biblical texts to confirm their patristic teaching. R. P. C. Hanson summarizes my conclusion.

> The baptismal creed in the early centuries is so meager and bare in its substance as to constitute no serious rival to or supplement of Scripture. Baptism, the Eucharist and the ministry [all] antedate the New Testament, *but without the New Testament our knowledge of them would be so uncertain and indefinite as to render them useless as vehicles of tradition.* As a source of original information *independent of Scripture*, tradition is useless [italics added].[5]

THE ROLE OF SCRIPTURE

Scripture plays the major role in the faith and practice of vital Christianity. It is always the starting point for dialogue about unity. I typically employ a simple way to engage this dialogue. I ask a group of people—ministers and priests in most cases—"Do we agree on the truths confessed in the Apostles' Creed?" (By the way, in every place I have found people who seriously fudge on this point. Destructive theological liberalism, along with ethical and moral compromise, will always be a serious problem.) After hearing their response, I can proceed to points of common agreement.

But evangelicals often treat the interpretation of Scripture as a purely scientific enterprise involving the right rules of grammar and logic. Exegesis has become the new "religious order." At its worst, this approach creates new forms of sectarianism and fails to hold a serious place for tradition in interpretation. Who needs tradition when you can read Greek and Hebrew—or listen to those who do? In this instance, the ordinary Christian is lost in the confusion of multiple interpretations. In much of the evangelical world, the individual is forced to pick. Their favorite teacher usually wins!

I increasingly find the evangelical reaction to tradition puzzling. The members of the early church handled the Scriptures with profound care. We would do well to consider their understanding of the sacred text. While some suggest that their allegorizing of Scripture disqualifies them as solid interpreters, I maintain that allegory can and should be used carefully like any other literary device.[6] There are some Scriptures that clearly indicate they are allegorical.

Evangelical "literalism" has produced some bitter fruit, the worst of which might be an inordinate and unwise use of the apocalyptic literature in the Bible. My mother, who was influenced by this kind of thinking, wrote in my first Bible, "If the literal sense makes good sense, seek no other sense, lest it result in nonsense." Applying the idea of a "literal" interpretation in such a manner robs Christians of the rich diet God has provided for them in the Holy Scripture, a diet that can be discovered much better with the help of the earliest Christian commentators and writers.

Because the early church writers were closer to the apostles and the development of the New Testament than we are, we ought to listen to them. I am grateful for the efforts undertaken by modern evangelical scholars to publish the insights of the ancient church, and I am excited to see academic undertakings in evangelical institutions that now address this issue. Such study centers and publishing projects have become venues where Catholic,

Orthodox, and Protestant Christians come to know God's truth as the one people of God.[7]

THE WISDOM OF THE CHURCH FATHERS

Why bother to read the church fathers? The British Congregational clergyman and scholar Erik Routley answers:

> It is profitable and exciting to read the fathers, if for no more exalted reason, because in them you find the church wrestling at every stage with questions that have concerned it in every generation since, and which are still concerning it now. Sometimes they are questions which the Scriptures are not designed to answer—questions subsidiary to the great controversy between God and his people, but none the less urgent questions. Nothing is lost, and I here hope something is positively gained, by returning to the early days and seeing what happened when these questions came for the first time before a learned and articulate Christian mind.
>
> But in any case I believe the responsible Christian is the better, and will know himself to be the better, for reading only a couple of pages of Athanasius or Origen. When these arguments strike him as familiar, he will have his notion of the communion of saints confirmed and illuminated, and when they strike him as strange or unusual, he will at least know himself to be conversing with, and learning from, some of the giants of the church's thought and devotion.[8]

In the introduction to a twentieth-century translation of an Athanasius classic, *The Incarnation of the Word of God*, C. S. Lewis stated that there was a "strange idea abroad that in every subject the ancient books should be read only by the professionals, and that the amateur should content himself with the modern books."[9] My appeal here is simple: The modern church desperately needs both ministers and nonprofessionals to read the patristic writers.

Christopher Hall, chancellor of Eastern University, has done yeoman's service in getting evangelicals into the ancient tradition. Hall adds:

> For the fathers, as for at least one of the three great ecclesiastical communions of the Christian world—Eastern

Orthodoxy—theology and spirituality, the Christian mind and heart, worship and reflection are an inseparable whole. The fathers continually remind us that theology is at best broken speech about the transcendent, mysterious God who draws near to us in the incarnation of the Son and the presence of the Spirit.[10]

This amazing quotation deserves to be read again and again. As I read the church fathers, I am reminded of the limitations of human language and of my self-centered perspective. In the words of an Eastern Orthodox writer, the West could profit from this stance since it tends to "avoid the essentially mysterious nature of Christianity ... rather than [to] adore it."[11]

WHAT IS GOING ON HERE?

A new sense of unity among Christians is forming around a common understanding of what is essential in Scripture. We have realized that unity does not come about by agreement on the interpretation of every verse or doctrine. As R. P. C. Hanson states, "An appreciation of the necessity, the limits, and proper function of tradition is essential for all parties in the ecumenical debate."[12]

Evangelicals can see tradition in a way that makes an important contribution when they enter the ongoing process in which the core values of Christian community are advanced through interpretive insights and serious reflection. University of Notre Dame senior research professor of philosophy Alasdair MacIntyre provides a helpful understanding of what this looks like:

A tradition is an argument extended through time in which certain fundamental agreements are defined and redefined in terms of two kinds of conflict: those with critics and enemies external to the tradition who reject all or at least key parts of those fundamental agreements, and those internal, interpretative debates through which the meaning and rationale of the fundamental agreements come to be expressed and by whose progress a tradition is constituted.[13]

Just as a person or family has a history and memory, so does the body of Christ. Tradition is nothing more or less than the means by which we understand this memory. This is how we know who we are as God's people. The New Testament itself came about through three centuries of life, reflection, and discussion.

DRAWING FROM THE DEEP WELL

Perhaps no modern Protestant theologian has done more to underscore our need for a postdenominational, flexible, and deeply rooted ancient faith than Thomas C. Oden, a lifelong Methodist. Oden, once a liberal seminary professor, consciously turned away from this ideology some years ago and in the process began to embrace the convergence of ancient orthodoxy with modern church renewal. Over the last twenty years, Tom has advocated a clear return to the tradition and orthodoxy of the ancient church.

In his brilliant book *The Rebirth of Orthodoxy: Signs of New Life in Christianity*, Oden points to what he sees as a transformation of character taking place in the lives of many Christians who are returning to ancient-faith patterns. He sees a rediscovery of early biblical interpretation and tradition in academic settings in which ancient writers are being read afresh. The wisdom of these writings is impacting an ever-widening circle of Christians as this rediscovery of ancient orthodoxy filters into the ecosystem of the church. Christians of all backgrounds are now drawing from this deep well.

As historical cultures worldwide are converging and cross-fertilizing, a new multicultural understanding of orthodoxy is creating an ecumenical consensus that respects both unity and diversity in entirely fresh ways. Oden suggests that a re-centering is also taking place within many of the congregations in the older Protestant denominations. Even some lapsed institutions and agencies are being affected through proactive efforts led by grassroots confessing movements. He maintains that these trends have resulted in a new commitment to classical ecumenism where Catholic, evangelical, and Orthodox bilateral conversations are now taking place.

This recovery of ecumenism follows the ancient ecumenical method of stressing consensual doctrinal integrity rather than modern denials of the faith. Dr. Oden provides extensive evidence that this multitextured movement is a resurgence of the type of orthodoxy that embraces "what has been believed everywhere, always, and by all."[14] I wholeheartedly agree with Oden regarding the impact of this resurgent theological movement he calls **paleo-orthodoxy.**[15]

THE GREAT EVANGELICAL CATASTROPHE

I do not wish to overdramatize my point, but evangelicalism's two-hundred-year approach to tradition has been an unmitigated disaster. Tradition has generally been seen by many evangelicals as an enemy. The former president of one of America's largest evangelical seminaries spoke for a large number of evangelicals when he wrote, "The very fact that I did not study a prescribed course in theology made it possible for me to approach the subject with an unprejudiced mind and to be concerned only with what the Bible actually teaches."[16] Following this approach has further divided churches and created a profound problem that is not solved by simple exegetical arguments.

Much of the modern evangelical movement has been built on schism—a schism rooted in an antitradition perspective. We thought this was the best way for a church to remain faithful.[17] A simple study of early church history would divest us of this idea. I am convinced that as long as we remain opposed to Christian tradition, we will never solve this problem. We will keep building churches on the foundation of strong human personalities and then follow these leaders, much as the Corinthians did with various teachers in their context (Paul, Peter, Apollos; see 1 Corinthians 1:10–17). We seem to have forgotten that the sovereign Lord has clearly stated, "I will not yield my glory to another" (Isaiah 42:8).

The result of this schism is a small view of the church and a big view of our own importance. We have exalted our interpretations of the Scripture by boldly proclaiming: "My authority comes only from the Bible." Thankfully, many are waking up to the tragedy of this false individualism and are wisely looking for help from the three great classical Christian traditions and the scores of ancient writers who feed their hunger. This is paleo-orthodoxy, and it drives a growing number of us to embrace a much bigger view of the church.

QUESTIONS FOR
DISCUSSION AND REFLECTION

1. Does the positive view of tradition in this chapter challenge the things you have been taught? What difference would it make if you saw tradition positively and gleaned new blessings from it?

2. How much does tradition impact your life? Who or what particular tradition has influenced you and how? Is this good or bad?

3. Have you read the church fathers? Do you think reading them could benefit your own spiritual formation? How could they help you hear Scripture?

4. Do you think an antitradition perspective has been a "great evangelical disaster"? If so, how has this affected your own life and church?

future

THE MISSIONAL-ECUMENICAL MOVEMENT

chapter fourteen

Searching for the True Church

The fact is that the differences between churches do matter. The question is not, "How can we overlook these differences?" but "How can we achieve a church which includes the many facets of the truth?" True catholicity is not obtained by overlooking differences but by accepting them and understanding them as a vital part of the nature of the church.

Robert E. Webber

DENOMINATIONS ARE CLEARLY NOT FOUND in the Bible, and it is time everyone admits this fact. Perhaps the only biblical analogy that comes close to our current situation is in Paul's discussion about worldliness in the church at Corinth.[1] One could compare Paul's language to our modern context and hear people saying, "I belong to John Calvin. I belong to John Wesley. I belong to Benedict XVI." And we can hear nondenominational Christians adding, "I belong to Christ!" Lesslie Newbigin argued that the existence of this type of plurality is an intolerable scandal. Newbigin rightly says that the rhetorical questions of 1 Corinthians 1:13 flow from the question, Is Christ divided?—questions that "show how any breach in the unity of the church was in violent contradiction to the very heart of the gospel as Paul understood it."[2]

So how should we understand denominations? They are groups of believers and/or churches united on the basis of a common set of beliefs and practices or a historical reality that shaped their formation and existence. But are these groups of churches a problem or a solution? Or to ask the question in a more provocative way,

Should we end all Protestant denominations and become independent Christians and churches? Or should we go back to Rome, whence we historically came? (Some Catholics, especially former Protestants, think so.) Or should we perhaps join the Orthodox Church in order to discover the one true church? If any of this were to actually happen—we are clearly imagining something beyond what we can conceive—would the results of this restructuring of Christians and congregations be good for the mission of Christ? Since I have argued that relational unity is what Jesus prayed for, I think it is appropriate that we take some time to delve deeper into the issue of denominations.

THE IDEAL CHURCH MISUNDERSTOOD

The fact that the church is one should be understood in at least two ways. In the ancient sense, oneness referred to *uniqueness*. Oneness was a statement about an ideal. It is rightly claimed that there is one church because there is one Lord. God has chosen out of the world's peoples a vast company of persons to make up one supernatural community.

Biblical scholar Luke Timothy Johnson, a Roman Catholic, makes this observation about the claim to uniqueness.

> It can easily be turned from a sense of witness to the world into a claim of privilege. On this basis, the church can claim to have replaced Israel as "God's elect people"—and has done so. It can disqualify the spiritual teachings of other religions on the basis of exclusive spiritual truth—and does so. And rival versions of the church can and do fight bitterly against each other to represent the "one" church of Christ worthy of that name. Although there is a certain truth to the ideal of a single church, it is an ideal that, when claimed as a reality, can become dangerous.[3]

The above comment will trouble sectarians. But Lesslie Newbigin is surely right:

> We do not find that our Lord first laid down a compendium of doctrine and then invited those who believed it to form an association on that basis. The personal fellowship and the doctrine were given together.... The divine society into

which [Jesus] admitted men was more than a school of correct theology. It was a personal fellowship of those who believed in him, who had yet many things to learn which they could only learn slowly and stumblingly, but who could be trusted to be his ambassadors to the world and the foundation stones of his church because they abode in him.[4]

THE IDEAL CHURCH UNDERSTOOD

There is, I believe, a correct way to understand the *ideal church*—thinking of it in the terms used by the apostle Paul.

> To the church of God in Corinth, to those sanctified in Christ Jesus and called to be his holy people, *together with all those everywhere who call on the name of the Lord Jesus Christ*, their Lord and ours:
>   Grace and peace to you from God our Father and the Lord Jesus Christ.
>
> *1 Corinthians 1:2–3, italics added*

This concept of the church of God occurs in Acts 20:28 and 2 Corinthians 1:1. The term has an Old Testament counterpart in the expression "assembly [or community] of the LORD" (see Deuteronomy 23:1). The church is God's community on earth. Paul says this ideal church is made up of *all people everywhere* "who call on the name of the Lord Jesus Christ."

It is helpful, though, to put a bold punctuation mark here. Neither Roman Catholic nor Orthodox Christians think of themselves as "denominations." Having noted there are necessary nuances in the term, I use it here in a generic sense to apply to common beliefs, practices, and forms of government found in a church or group of churches. I mean no disrespect.

Since Vatican II, Roman Catholic theology has referred to non-Catholics as "separated brethren." This is a great improvement over what was taught before 1960. But Rome still claims to be *the* true (ideal) church. The ideal church is thus still understood as consisting somehow in Rome's hierarchy and structure. The bishops are the successors of the apostles, and the pope is Peter's successor. This understanding is then connected to a valid administration of the sacraments.

Orthodoxy has a different view. It sees the church as a mystical entity that comprises God's direct activity. One Orthodox theologian states that the church is "the will of God manifesting itself in the world."[5] Orthodox Christians generally place more stress on the divine character of the church than Protestants do. In Orthodoxy, the church is both the fullness of the life of the Holy Spirit and the body of Christ, understood *spiritually* and *sacramentally*. The end result is this: Orthodoxy sees itself as the visible church of Jesus Christ in historical continuity with the earliest Christian assemblies. It may not use the word *true* in precisely the way it is used in the West, but it thinks of itself as *the* one church.

A commonly used statement given to me by my Orthodox friends expresses their understanding: "It is the work of the church to say where the church *is*; it is not the work of the church to say where it is *not*." In this view, Orthodoxy believes it constitutes the one visible church in continuity with Christ and his apostles, but the church does not determine who is a true Christian.

Anthony Ugolnik, a Greek Orthodox priest of Russian heritage and a professor at a non-Orthodox university in America, helps us understand Orthodoxy in this regard: "We Christians of America and Russia, simply by reaching a greater understanding of how each of us envisions and lives the gospel, can live the gospel more fully. If we cut ourselves off from that understanding, reject it, or mutilate it through our suspicion or hatred, we are turning ourselves away from God's grace."[6]

Ugolnik realizes that there is an **ontological** reality we should call the *true* church. He believes Orthodoxy is that church. But he also says that far from isolating ourselves from each other, we should move toward "loving association" with Christians everywhere.[7] The reason is that the Christian faith is relational.

EVERYONE WHO CALLS ON THE NAME OF THE LORD

No matter how we understand our past and present differences, we should agree that the church includes "everyone who calls on the name of the Lord" (Acts 2:21). I suggest this must be our starting point. Our present state remains formally divided, but a lot of the work of the kingdom is actually carried out in informal contexts.

There is an additional way to understand the church's oneness. Oneness can be seen as a claim about what the church is in itself—"The church is one because it lives a life of real unity."[8] This picture is painted by Luke in his account of the early church in Acts 2:44: "All the believers were together and had everything in common." Luke later writes, "All the believers were one in heart and mind" (Acts 4:32). This seems to be the same unity Paul urges in Ephesians 4:3–6. But in the verses that follow (4:7–12), Paul argues that there should also be diversity. Luke Timothy Johnson writes, "Paul also allows for a diversity of practice in matters that are not critical to the identity of the community."[9]

The simple truth is this: *Unity is not uniformity.* I am convinced that the presence of the Holy Spirit guarantees both unity and diversity. As believers, we share in the unity of the Trinity, and so we should have the same way of thinking that was expressed in Jesus' relationship with his Father. Their unity was complete, but we only know incompletely: "Now we see only a reflection as in a mirror; then we shall see face to face. Now I know in part; then I shall know fully, even as I am fully known" (1 Corinthians 13:12).

So how should the unity and diversity seen within the Trinity impact our relationships? I suggest we consider more deeply how each member in the Trinity cares for the other with love and tenderness.[10] Such a social and relational understanding of the Trinity will impact profoundly how we treat each other if we put it into practice.

The church has confessed this unique Trinitarian oneness from earliest times—but this is clearly not how we have lived. Unity has generally been institutionalized as sameness. Or it has been forced by the sword. History shows the church reeling from two extremes—uniformity and deviance. When uniformity goes too far, we oppress and suppress those who disagree with us; when deviance goes too far, we allow almost anything that our age deems appropriate. Unity in Christ and the truth must be our pattern. Uniformity is not healthy. But some forms of diversity must be understood as illegitimate too or the church's mission is adversely harmed, which is precisely what I submit is happening in America today.

The church is wrestling mightily with questions about sexual ethics. The question often comes down to this: Is the modern world driving the agenda, or is it Scripture and our ancient/future faith? If we grasp both unity and diversity, we should ask, How does the ethical teaching of Scripture, rooted in the gospel of Christ, define the church's moral and spiritual life? Be prepared for a difficult struggle without simplistic answers.

IN ESSENTIALS UNITY, IN NONESSENTIALS FREEDOM, IN ALL THINGS CHARITY

A famous dictum is still useful: "In essentials, unity; in nonessentials, freedom; and in all things, charity." But a great problem remains—one Christian's "nonessential" is another's "essential." This is why I have made such a concerted effort to push us back to the Scriptures and the earliest ecumenical creeds. These will not solve everything, but these standards provide a historical context. Having said this, I concur with Lesslie Newbigin, who writes, "What God has done for us in Christ, what we have to rely on, is much more than we can formulate in detailed statements or appropriate in conscious religious experience."[11]

This requires a "hermeneutic of generosity." We must lovingly read Scripture together if we want to preserve a proper balance between unity and diversity. I've learned along the way that there is no quick fix to schism. Newbigin got it right: "The world will always, consciously or unconsciously, judge what the church says by what it is. They will interpret the printed epistle by the living epistle."[12]

DENOMINATIONALISM AND CATHOLICITY: CAN THEY COEXIST?

The famous American church historian Winthrop Hudson wrote, "Denominationalism is the opposite of sectarianism."[13] I had to read this statement several times to make sure I understood it. I thought, "He must be kidding." I soon discovered he was not. His reasons frame my answer to the problem of denominations.

Some years ago, a T-shirt showed up on various seminary campuses. On it was imprinted a checklist of theological and denominational differences with the following categories:

- ☐ Dispensationalist
- ☐ Ultra-dispensationalist
- ☐ Calvinist
- ☐ 5 point
- ☐ 4 point
- ☐ 3 point

- ☐ Covenant Theologian
- ☐ Wesleyan Perfectionist
- ☐ Arminian
- ☐ Pentecostal (First Wave)
- ☐ Charismatic (Second Wave)
- ☐ Neo-charismatic (Third Wave)

☐ Plain Ol' Christian

If you are like me you are probably tired of these labels. You just want to be a "plain ol' Christian." If only it were that easy. But there is one major problem with being a plain ol' Christian. You must eventually come to grips with what the Bible teaches and how you are going to follow Jesus and then love those who disagree with you. You will soon learn that some of the most difficult Christians to get along with are plain ol' Christians. While this label sounds good, it is not a serious option unless you deny the Christian reality of all those who lived before you. So ending denominations will not solve the problem of disunity any more than uniting them into a federated church will solve it. I think Winthrop Hudson knew this.

Are denominations helpful or harmful to pursuing the unity of Christians? I do not believe denominations are the formal problem, though often they are a real problem. If we address the real problem, we can pursue a unity that is visible and missional. Denominations may die or radically change, but the church will remain until Jesus Christ returns.

In many ways Protestant denominations resemble what evangelicals call parachurch missions. Because we need to translate the Holy Scriptures into hundreds of languages, we have an agency such as Wycliffe Bible Translators. Because churches need accountability, we have denominations to help us meet this need. I believe Protestant denominations are irregular but not invalid. While they may help us pursue obedience to the mission of Christ, we ought to recognize that there is much more to our unity than these structures.

The answer is not found in a nondenominational approach either, since this creates new denominations, whether one single church or a few like-minded churches. Denominations are sub-biblical, interim structures. I believe we should pray that this whole arrangement might be wonderfully altered by the sovereign work of the Spirit.

THE UNITY WE SEEK TO MANIFEST

My denomination has adopted a statement that summarizes my understanding of unity:

> The Reformed Church in America believes God calls forth through his Holy Spirit from among lost men a people—his church—whom he commissions to proclaim to the world his gospel of Christ's redemption.
>
> This calling and commissioning belong to one church, a united fellowship, having one Lord, one faith, one baptism, one God and Father, which is commissioned with one task to the human race.
>
> We believe our task is the proclamation of the gospel of Jesus Christ as we worship the Lord when we hear his word and celebrate his sacraments, as we witness to the mighty acts of God in history, and as we serve the world with a ministry of love.
>
> In obedience to this divine revelation, we of the Reformed Church in America resolve to manifest the God-given unity of the church by working to overcome our divisions. The ways and means to unity are not always known. The goal of our unity is a venture of faith. Therefore, trusting in the Holy Spirit for guidance, we shall be open to his counsel, willing to converse with any church, ready to cooperate with all Christians, committed to participate in councils of church on all levels, prepared to merge with any church when it is clearly the will of God, eager to heal the brokenness of

the body of Christ in all ways made known to us, until all are one, so that the world may know that the Father has sent the Son as Savior and Lord.

Adopted by the General Synod of the Reformed Church in America, 1966

THE DANGERS OF LOSING THE CATHOLICITY OF DENOMINATIONALISM

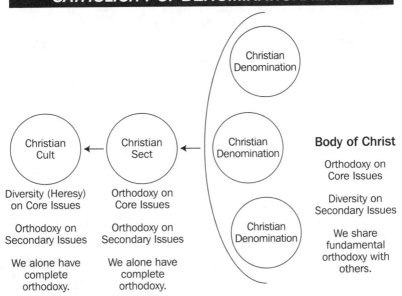

FIGURE 14.1 Taken from Rex Koivisto, *One Lord, One Faith* (2nd ed.; Eugene, Ore.: Wipf & Stock, 2009), 111. Used by permission of Wipf and Stock Publishers. *www.wipfandstock.com*

WHICH CHURCH IS THE ONE TRUE CHURCH?

Time and again I have seen serious attempts to pursue biblical unity broken down by the absolute certitude that we know what constitutes the *true* church. While I was writing this book, a brochure arrived inviting me to a "True Church Conference." The program was evangelical, with an emphasis on doctrine, theology, application, evangelism, and mentoring. The event was sponsored by a "truth-driven association of churches." I wonder how we will ever move beyond the question of the true church as long as theology is understood in this way.

Lesslie Newbigin offers a beautiful alternative. He believed that the one church never ceased to exist, even though it was defaced and divided by sin. Like the Corinthian church, this church has not been divided into one true fellowship with a bunch of (untrue) counterfeit groups. What we really have are mutually compromised factions with continuing, legitimate ecclesiological claims on one another. Simply put, schism does not annihilate God's presence in the various fellowships.[14]

When we correctly understand our distinctions, we actually help preserve some of the hard-won strengths the whole church needs (for example, the emphasis on grace that was recovered and highlighted by the Protestant Reformers). But our resulting schism compromised God's grace since no one group can ever live up to the full promise of the whole church. As a result, our factions afflict both our internal health and our external witness.

This diagnosis challenges false opposites in this debate about the true church. On the one hand, we must resist the exclusivism of any single position—Roman Catholic, Orthodox, Magisterial Protestant, or "Pentecostal" (Free)—that claims for itself the totality of grace and truth; on the other hand, this approach resists the inclusivism that adds up the totality of various traditions to create a federation resulting in compromised pluralism. Duke Divinity School theology professor Geoffrey Wainwright sums up what happened in his own experience: "After Newbigin, I have stopped searching for the One True Church, for he has helped me see that I already belong to it."[15]

QUESTIONS FOR
DISCUSSION AND REFLECTION

1. How can a sectarian understanding of the church misuse the concept of an "ideal church"? How can we think of the ideal church correctly?

2. Can we enter into serious dialogue about unity with Catholic and Orthodox believers if they believe they are the true church? What limitations are placed on our fellowship by our different views of the church?

3. Do you think we can use the biblical phrase "everyone who calls on the name of Lord" as an elemental starting point for our attempts at visible unity and missional cooperation? Why or why not?

4. What problems do you see in reducing all of our Christian differences to being "plain ol' Christians"? How do evangelicals fail to grasp the importance of the doctrine of the church at this point?

chapter fifteen

Who Is a Real Christian?

A Christian is a person in whom God is working by his grace, according to his promises in Christ Jesus. There is no such thing as a Christian in whose heart God is not working.

Manford G. Gutzke

Men are not born Christians but become such.

Tertullian

It is fitting then, not only to be called Christians, but to be so in reality. For it is not the being called so, but the being really so, that renders a man blessed.

Ignatius

THE NAME *CHRISTIAN* seems to have arisen in the early church as a nickname, much like people today are called Methodists, Baptists, or Lutherans. Luke states, "The disciples were called Christians first at Antioch" (Acts 11:26). The term must have caught on quickly since at Paul's interrogation by a Roman governor, he was asked, "Do you think that in such a short time you can persuade me to be a Christian?" (Acts 26:28). The only other use of the term in the New Testament occurs when Peter refers to the hardships of believers as suffering "as a Christian" (1 Peter 4:16). Peter's use is the only time the term describes fellow believers. Perhaps there is a touch of irony here since the term *Christian* was likely an accusation.

The New Testament has a number of designations for Christ-followers. They were people of "the Way" (Acts 9:2; 19:9), which perhaps captures the sense of John 14:6. They are also called those who "follow God's example" (Ephesians 5:1; "imitators," 1 Thessalonians 1:6) and "believers" (Acts 5:12; 9:30; 1 Timothy 4:10). The most common New Testament terms used to designate believers were "the Lord's people" (NIV, "saints," Acts 9:32; Romans 15:25), "the elect" (Mark 13:27; 2 Timothy 2:10), "brothers and sisters" (Romans 16:14; Ephesians 6:23), and "the disciples" (Acts 11:26, 29). In Acts, they were accused of being part of "the Nazarene sect" (24:5), which could only have significant meaning within Palestine where the term had a pejorative connotation.

Within one generation of the time the name *Christian* was first used in Antioch, the term had become common. By AD 64, during the reign of Nero, the Roman historian Tacitus referred to believers as "Christians." Soon the term was embraced by those who followed Christ. "By the middle of the second century it had been taken up as one of jubilant testimony by those who might have expected martyrdom if they admitted to being a follower of Jesus Christ."[1]

The term had appropriate meaning for early Christians since the Greek word *christos* meant "anointed." With an *ian* suffix, it meant "similar to" Christ. Christ is the uniquely anointed one of God, and his followers were anointed by his Spirit. John writes of Christians, "You have an anointing from the Holy One, and all of you know the truth" (1 John 2:20). John also refers to "the anointing you received from him" (2:27). The term may have arisen from outside the church but it was embraced by those on the inside. It appears that the early Christians differentiated themselves from the Jews and the pagans by the use of the term *Christian*, much like we use it today to distinguish Christians from Muslims, Hindus, or Buddhists.

In defining a Christian, a simple answer works best: *A Christian is someone who believes in Jesus Christ as Lord and Savior and follows his teachings.*

NOMINAL CHRISTIANS

When I held tenaciously to sectarianism, I continually wrestled with this question: Who is a real Christian? I wanted to know who was real and who was not. I believed some who professed to be Christians were not real disciples.

This question is, in one sense, quite complex. Those who teach missions write about "nominal Christians." The Lausanne Committee defined nominal Christians as "those who, within the Protestant tradition, would call themselves Christian, or be so regarded by others, but who have *no authentic commitment to Christ based on personal faith* (italics added)."[2] Often Christians of the second and third generation grow up without vital faith. All three of the great traditions of Christianity recognize the problem, though each has a different response.

The evangelical approach, expressed at Lausanne, suggests there are five types of nominal Christians:

- those who attend church regularly and worship devoutly without a personal relationship with Christ
- those who attend church regularly for cultural reasons
- those who attend church only for major church events
- those who hardly ever attend church but maintain a church relationship for reasons of security, emotional or family ties, or tradition
- those who have no specific relationship with any church and never attend but consider themselves Christians

No one can seriously doubt that all five of these types exist. A simple reading of the biblical evidence is enough to make thoughtful Christians doubt that all of those who say they believe in Jesus Christ are real Christians. A challenge for healthy churches will always be the problem of how to move nominal Christians into a vibrant, living, personal relationship with Jesus Christ.

PROCLAMATION AND PARTICIPATION

The New Testament provides an adequate answer to the question, Who is a Christian? And I believe that accepting this perspective will combat sectarianism. Paul writes, "If anyone does not have the Spirit of Christ, they do not belong to Christ" (Romans 8:9). Pretty clear, isn't it? Those who have the Spirit of Christ are his, and those who do not are not.

Consider how *The Message* paraphrases this in its larger context:

> If God himself has taken up residence in your life, you can hardly be thinking more of yourself than of him. Anyone, of course, who has not welcomed the invisible but clearly present God, the Spirit of Christ, won't know what we're talking about. But for you who welcome him, in whom he dwells—even though you still experience all the limitations of sin—you yourself experience life on God's terms.
>
> *Romans 8:9–10*

Unmistakably true Christians have the Spirit of God. In its note on Romans 8:9, *The Orthodox Study Bible* states, "The Spirit of Christ declares the intimacy between the Son and the Holy Spirit. The Son becomes incarnate by the Holy Spirit (Mark 1:20) and in turn sends the Holy Spirit from the Father into the world (John 15:26; 16:7).[3]

Remember where the first believers were called Christians? Antioch. Much more than simply being a historical marker in Luke's story, he reveals that the disciples had obeyed their Lord and the gospel had penetrated into the Gentile world, reaching into the great city of Antioch. John Chrysostom (AD 347–407) apparently recognized the significance: "It was there in the first place that men were accounted worthy of that name."[4]

We know that two primary events were central to the life of the early church—assembly at the Lord's Supper and the teaching of the gospel. The early church accepted into its company those who professed faith and were baptized. (I will not address the question of baptizing children since it is not relevant here.) These baptized Christians gathered at the Lord's Table and heard the gospel. This is proclamation and participation.

THE SECTARIAN CHALLENGE

I believe sectarianism breeds a radically different response to the problem of nominal Christianity. The sectarian response must be rejected as a deadly, zero-sum enterprise, as something that destroys the witness of the church and corrupts relationships.

We often hear prominent conservative Christians assure us that "so-and-so is not a real Christian!" Christians feel bound to attack a person for holding a view they believe to be theologically wrong. They discover on the Internet some tidbit that feeds their paranoia about the false teachers in the world. Christian publishers ought to know better, but time and again they allow authors to slander fellow Christians without impunity. We have heard a lot about culture wars in the United States for thirty years. I am far more concerned about the truth wars waged by polemicists inside the church. This is the bitter fruit of sectarianism. It lacks charity and leads to mean-spiritedness.

Privately, I hear people ask, "Who is a real Christian?" with regard to their own family members or members of their congregations (including pastors). If a Catholic becomes an evangelical, then those who remain Catholic are viewed by the "convert" as non-Christians. (Remember, just being Catholic, Protestant, or Orthodox does not mean "Christ's Spirit lives in you.") Some of my harshest critics are former Catholics who are now fervent evangelicals. There is a similar response when a Protestant converts to Catholicism, often with great rejoicing that this person is now a "Catholic" Christian. A fervent Catholic apologist may even declare that this person has finally been united with Christ. These Catholics disagree with the better instincts of their own church.

I am wearied by this attempt to say who is and is not a real Christian. My guess is that many of you are too. I find it destructive of everything true to Christ's teaching. During my journey to catholicity, I made a conscious choice to give up this approach. After all, if a Christian is someone who has "the Spirit of Christ," then I do not know who truly has "the Spirit of Christ." Scripture further declares, "The Lord knows those who are his" (2 Timothy 2:19). My choice to drop out of this deadly dialogue was liberating. I ceased being a judge. Real conversion and true faith are God's work. And since all three of the great traditions of Christianity teach that those who share in proclamation and participation must also have explicit living faith, I began to openly encourage explicit faith rather than wage attacks on others.

Once I took this step, I became more concerned about my own faith and attitudes. I no longer had to answer many of the questions people asked me about other people—questions that only fed my pride. I ask, "Why should you care about what I think since I don't know the real answer?" I then ask, "Have you confessed faith in Christ? Are you his baptized follower?" If the answer is affirmative, then I proclaim the gospel and let the Spirit work as he wills. God will judge the heart. As for the category of nominal Christians, I believe this idea is useful for mission purposes, but I have chosen to reject it in my own evaluation of which persons I will associate with and how I speak about them.

This practice of judging others will always ruin the true fellowship (*koinonia*) Christ died for. There is a right way to disagree with other Christians—truth expressed in love. "Who are you to judge someone else's servant? To their own master they stand or fall" (Romans 14:4).

HERE COMES THE JUDGE

In his earnest plea for God to save the wicked city of Sodom, Abraham asks the rhetorical question, "Will not the Judge of all the earth do right?" (Genesis 18:25)—rooted in Abraham's confidence that the justice of God guarantees he will do right. Let's leave judgment to God and embrace a big view of the church that stops the cynical response.

So is there any judgment that Christians should make about whether or not a person is a real Christian? I understand the New Testament to teach that such judgment is a church matter, not a private one. Faithful shepherds are responsible for the souls of people in their care. But even good shepherds will never render perfect judgment. If people need a warning, there is a correct way to deliver it. Look to the Pastoral Epistles and the deep resources of spiritual formation. This type of ministry can be done well by wise leaders who earnestly labor in such demanding work (see Matthew 7:1–6). And if people need corrective church discipline, there is a proper way to administer it as well (see Matthew 18:15–20).

In my opinion, the way most Christians publicly speak about who is and is not a Christian is condemned by Scripture. But this practice is advanced by teachers who routinely defend truth and expose error. I believe the Scriptures reveal that godly leaders should expose false teachers, especially if their teaching denies core orthodoxy. (The category of heresy still matters when properly used.) But this does not mean we should adopt the polemics of mutually assured destruction (MAD).

Some years ago, a friend shared a story about harsh attacks on Dr. Billy Graham in his early days of ministry. Many of these attacks came from former friends. His soul was vexed, but he determined to never fight back. His goal was to bless those Christians who attacked him. On one significant occasion, a major leader violated the work of Dr. Graham in a way that was particularly egregious. Dr. Graham hastily called a board meeting. He made it clear that there would be no counterattack. The board then prayed for the other minister, and the issue was dropped.

When I first heard this story, it came as a lightning bolt of hope. I prayed that in my times of dealing with personal attacks, I would know half the grace that Dr. Graham knew. I thus strive to follow the clear command of my Lord: "Bless those who curse you, pray for those who mistreat you" (Luke 6:28).

CONCLUSION

I have found real Christians in every church I have ever entered. Even in the most ill-taught churches, I have discovered people who truly love the Lord Jesus Christ. I still have disagreements with certain churches and Christian teachers, but the way to live out my faith in love is to pursue the common good of all who follow Christ. This means I no longer spend precious time attacking other Christians.

QUESTIONS FOR DISCUSSION AND REFLECTION

1. How does the New Testament define a Christian? Should we use man-made criteria because we are familiar with them?
2. Do you think the designation "nominal Christian" is helpful? How can it be misused?
3. A true Christian has the "Spirit of Christ" in him or her. Such a person will give some evidence that he or she loves Christ, but this evidence will always be mixed. How can we guard against becoming "fruit inspectors" and spending time trying to decide who is a real Christian?

chapter sixteen

The Missional-Ecumenical Church

Christian mission gives expression to the dynamic relationship between God and the world.

David Bosch

The church is more than meets the eye. It is more than a set of well-managed functions. It is more than another human organization. The church lives in the world as a human enterprise, but it is also the called and redeemed people of God. It is a people of God who are created by the Spirit to live as a missionary people.

Craig Van Gelder

THE TERM *MISSIONAL CHURCH* has become a veritable buzzword — a most unfortunate turn of events, because the truth expressed by this word runs the risk of being co-opted by various movements within the larger church when in reality *missional* is a quality the entire church needs in the twenty-first century.

The mission of the church is not to solve society's problems or to gain political influence in order to change culture. And as important as adding members to a church is, recruiting new members for the church is not the church's mission either. The mission of the church is "to participate in the reconciling love of the triune God who reaches out to a fallen world in Jesus Christ and by the power of the Holy Spirit brings strangers and enemies into God's new and abiding community."[1]

Mission is not what *we* do so much as what *Jesus Christ* is doing in seeking and saving the lost (Luke 19:10) through us. Our part is to discover our unique context and calling within the larger community so that we can be an active part of Christ's mission. A missional church is powerfully shaped by the incarnation and the holy Trinity and exists to *be* Christ's mission, not simply to *support* mission(s). A missional church will never be satisfied simply to send people overseas or give sums of money for mission programs.

It should be more apparent than ever that nothing may be as detrimental to the mission of Christ as the disunity of Christians. A significant resurgence of interest in reconnecting the authority of Scripture with the immensely valuable resource of Christian tradition is fostering a bigger vision of the church. But this resurgence will lose its momentum if it is not vitally linked to Christ's mission. I believe the link we need is found in what I call missional-ecumenism. This approach is already bringing about a new reformation in our discourse about the church and Christ's mission and may yet bring about a new reformation in our practice if Christian leaders hear this message and act on it.

A little over a decade ago, a research project conducted by theologians deeply interested in the mission of the church generated an important book titled *Missional Church*.[2] The team worked to define solutions to some of the issues I have focused on in this book. In the process, they coined the valuable word *missional*. These contributors agreed with the language of Vatican II, which stated, "The pilgrim church is missionary by her very nature."[3] The idea that the church is "missionary by her very nature" is the critical reason for using and understanding the word *missional*. I believe when we grasp the real significance of this term, we are forced to understand how the character of God and the nature of the church are eternally related.

Darrell L. Guder, professor of missional and ecumenical theology at Princeton Theological Seminary, describes the choice of the word *missional* this way: "We needed, somehow, to find a way to talk about the fundamentally missional nature of the church without using terms freighted with all kinds of baggage."[4] This thinking has formed a working consensus for an important new movement in theology that began in 1998.

UNITY: THE SIGN AND INSTRUMENT OF CHRIST'S MISSION

Lesslie Newbigin writes, "The church is both holy and sinful. This is the fundamental root of the whole problem of the church, that it is a union of sinful souls with the holy God."[5] But this "holy and sinful" church points all nations to the kingdom of Christ. We have seen that the church's unity is always in order because this is how the world will come to believe the message of Christ. The bond between our unity and the accomplishment of Christ's mission is very clear, but it has never gone uncriticized.

The most common disagreement with my thesis is that it is too pragmatic. If I were saying we can bring about unity in order to reach larger numbers of people, then I believe this criticism is valid. But this is *not* what I am saying. Lesslie Newbigin is again insightful.

> No doubt, as C. S. Lewis has so vividly suggested, the incarnation of the Son of God must have appeared to the pure spirituality of hell a most shocking and degrading episode, but it governs the nature of the church, which is the continuation of that mission to the world.... We must not define the church *simply* in terms of its mission.... The church ... cannot be defined in merely functional terms. But neither can it be described apart from the mission in which it has its being.... The church's unity is the sign and the instrument of the salvation which Christ has wrought and whose final fruition is the summing-up of all things in Christ.[6]

What Newbigin is arguing is important. The unity of the church is "the sign and the instrument" of Christ's mission. A disunited church is a direct and public contradiction of the gospel of the kingdom. When she is not a servant-bride, joined in unity for the salvation of the world, the church will substitute a partial message of good news for the richer biblical version. Newbigin expresses this far better than I can when he writes, "As we face the challenge which such encounter addresses to the things we hold most precious, we are compelled to face again the ultimate secret of the church's being, which is life-through-death in Christ."[7] Simply put, the mystery of the church's true fellowship is found in the life of Christ. By dying, he lived. When the church dies to her scandalous disunity, she will live by the power of the Holy Spirit.

SURVIVALISM AND TRIUMPHALISM

The separatism found in almost every American church context renders the gospel of the kingdom less and less attractive in our age. The missiologist Arthur F. Glasser wrote of the impact of this separatism on another land where American influence is obvious: "One cannot believe that the more than 125 separate societies serving in Japan alone can be viewed as an answer to our Lord's Prayer 'that they may all be one.' " The late Ugandan bishop Festo Kivengere said, "By our denominationalism we tell the world how much we hate each other." He considered the problem second only to apartheid as a hindrance to the gospel in South Africa.[8] I heartily agree with the concerns of these leaders, and it is why I have given my life to work and pray for the unity of Christ's church.

The influence of the fiercest forms of separatism seems to have waned in the last two decades in America. I find younger Christians are tired of it. This is good news. But the bad news is that some of these same young Christians seem ambivalent about Christian doctrine and tradition at critical points. I believe the answer to this problem is to recover classical Christianity in all of its paleo-orthodox forms. If we do not rediscover the Christian doctrine of God, these young leaders could soon flounder on the shoals of spiritual shipwreck. But this recovery of classical Christianity must proceed in the context of missional-ecumenism.

On one end of the spectrum, many older churches are in decline. For a time conservative churches seemed to have captured the field, but recent data suggests that these churches are now in decline as well. In both contexts, I submit that the church as a vital expression of Christ's life among Christians must become important again. At the end of the day, the church in the West continues to experience spiritual and moral decline. I believe we now face two great extremes—*survivalism* and *triumphalism*. In both cases the problem is clear: *the church is too small*. The gap between these extremes is often filled by leaders who do not care deeply enough about our unity. For many in my generation, what matters is "the church of what's happening now." Thankfully, there are wonderful exceptions, seen in a growing number of emerging leaders in both mainline (older) and conservative (newer) churches. My prayer is that God will make these exceptions the rule. "Lord, haste the day!"

JOHN R. MOTT AND THE RISE OF MISSIONAL-ECUMENISM

One of the best ways to understand a biblical concept is to hear it through the life of a faithful person. John R. Mott (1865–1955) was such a person—one of the fathers of the modern ecumenical movement. Mott's story inspires me to faithfulness. In his life the various strands of my book find clear expression.

While a student at Cornell University, John R. Mott underwent a marvelous conversion from agnosticism to deep evangelical faith when he heard an address by the famous C. T. Studd, a member of the "Cambridge Seven"—a group of English undergraduate athletes dedicated to foreign missions. Shortly after Mott's conversion, he began his life's work in mission.

Oliver Tomkins makes this observation about Mott:

> In the cause of world evangelization, Mott was as tireless and as urgent as the apostle Paul—and as careful to follow up initial visits by continuing contact. He traveled repeatedly to Asia and Africa long before air travel made such journeying commonplace.... Mott was an example of his own dictum about arranging a visit or a conference: "Plan as if there were no such thing as prayer. Pray as if there were no such thing as planning."[9]

John Mott was not initially a champion for Christian unity. What made him an ecumenical Christian was his deep passion for mission, as he came to realize that more was needed than mere cooperation. An urgency for ecumenism became Mott's vision after the World Student Christian Federation, founded by Mott, came in contact with Eastern Orthodox churches and student movements that were confessional and yet very different from

Mott's own pietistic Methodist background. Meeting Christians of different persuasions and ethnic backgrounds led to profound changes in his life, as has happened in mine as well. At the WSCF meeting in Nyborg in 1925, various confessional student movements were invited to become members of the federation, which led to a vital connection between interdenominational and denominational groups and to a growing interest in ecumenism. Mott played a major role in the first two world conferences on Faith and Order (Lausanne in 1927 and Edinburgh in 1937).

All of this led Mott to become involved in efforts for international peace, which culminated in his reception of the Nobel Peace Prize in 1946. When the World Council of Churches (WCC) held its inaugural meeting, the eighty-three-year-old Mott preached at the opening service. In his message, he said, "We have entered the most exciting period in the history of the church. It will take all the statesmanship, all the churchmanship, and all the self-forgetfulness of all of us. But to those who believe in the adequacy of Christ no doors are closed and boundless opportunities are open."[10] I keep this statement before me every day.

So what do we make of Mott's work more than fifty years after his death? One thing stands out—he was a visionary who cared about missional-ecumenism more than anything else. He never lost his zeal to see people come to know Christ as their Lord. His deep commitment to mission drove him. He was one of the first modern Christian leaders to see how passion for mission should be vitally connected to prayer for the unity of the whole church. Had the World Council of Churches labored with statesmanship, churchmanship, and self-forgetfulness, I wonder what might have happened. Sadly, most evangelicals never grasped Mott's vision. Another generation would pass before evangelical Protestants began to play a major role in worldwide efforts for Christian unity. Much of their energy until the 1970s was spent on negative reactions to ecumenism.[11]

THE LIFE OF LESSLIE NEWBIGIN (1909–1998)

As I noted earlier, Lesslie Newbigin has had the most influence on my understanding of mission and ecumenism. Bishop Newbigin was one of the leading ecumenical theological leaders of the twentieth century. His impact on my life is so profound that I require Christian leaders I equip, as well as students in the classes I teach, to immerse themselves in Newbigin's writings.

James Edward Lesslie Newbigin, born in Newcastle-upon-Tyne (England), made massive contributions to the church in the areas of missions, apologetics, and ecumenism. He was trained for the Presbyterian ministry at Cambridge and then appointed by the Church of Scotland for missionary service in South India in 1936. During World War II he helped bring about the union of several different churches into one new church—the Church of South India (CSI)—inaugurated in 1947. In 1948, he participated in the first World Council of Churches meeting in Amsterdam as a practitioner with strong theological insights. (This was the same gathering where John Mott gave the keynote address.) He remained a strong voice for mission and orthodoxy for a lifetime.

In 1959, Newbigin returned to England as the secretary of the International Missionary Council. He was the associate general secretary of the World Council of Churches and the director of the Commission on World Mission and Evangelism until 1965. After returning to India and serving as the bishop of the CSI until 1974, he lectured in a British college, became moderator of the general assembly of the United Reformed Church, and then (remarkably) served as the pastor of a small inner-city church (1980–1988). In the last twenty years of his full life, his legacy was solidified by a number of important books that provided a way to move away from the extremes of both liberalism and anti-ecumenical conservatism.

When I first began to read Lesslie Newbigin, I was impressed by his clear thought and the utter Christlikeness of the way he lived as a humble servant. Geoffrey Wainwright, who knew him well, wrote, "From my first meeting with him in 1963 to my last meeting with him late in 1996, the physical and mental impression he made on me was one of disciplined energy." Wainwright quotes a bishop of the Church of England, who said, "Lesslie in the flesh was quite as alluring as Lesslie in print." Wainwright adds, "As they met him in various arenas, many people sensed that the driving force was the Holy Spirit."[12]

In all honesty, the entire perspective of this book is shaped by this man. We all need role models, and when God dramatically shook my life in the early 1990s, this man quickly became mine. I am sorry I never had the joy of meeting him, though several of my friends had that privilege. Newbigin was unique because he was both an academician and a practitioner, an all-too-rare combination.

LEARNING TO THINK MISSIONALLY

The goal of Lesslie Newbigin was to challenge Western Christianity to rethink mission in a culture that had rejected Christendom. Traditional studies in missions, at least until the 1960s, were mostly motivational, inspirational, and promotional. The 1950s had produced a serious challenge to the old colonialist assumptions of Christendom and opened doors to new ways of thinking about mission, but a new day was on the horizon.

The famous archbishop of Canterbury, William Temple (1881–1944), called the reality of the multicultural global church "the great new fact of our time." If this was true when he said it more than sixty years ago, how much more true is it since World War II? The missional concept has spawned a discussion that challenges previous paradigms—paradigms that saw mission almost entirely as extending the church into unreached areas. The word *missional* represents a fresh, profoundly theological, and immensely practical way to think about the church in a time of transition. While Darrell Guder admits there is "terminological confusion" associated with this word, what ultimately matters is not the word itself.[13] What really matters in the end is a healthy response to the nature of Christ's church and the reality of its future.

Guder expresses the value of thinking missionally:

> Rather than seeing mission as, at best, one of the necessary prongs of the church's calling, and at worst as a misguided adventure, it must be seen as the fundamental, the essential, the centering understanding of the church's purpose and action. The church that Jesus intended ... is missional by its very nature. The church that the triune God gathers, upbuilds, and sends ... exists to continue the service of witness."[14]

MY CALL FOR MISSIONAL REFORMATION

From the time I was a young minister, I have believed strongly in biblical reformation. Reformation seeks to correct faults and defects so the church will be more faithful to Christ. There have been numerous reform movements throughout church history. But I do not believe in ecclesial revolutions or in the kind of radical change that overthrows what exists. Revolution wastes precious human resources and institutions and fosters sectarianism. Newer reform movements are often tugged in this direction out of a desire to get back to the Bible or to the first-century church. A healthy respect for historical theology and Christian tradition will correct this tendency.

When I first grasped this message of missional-ecumenism, I began to teach leaders and churches how to embrace spiritual renewal as a missional reformation. I am convinced this is the only reformation that will truly change the church in our postmodern context. My experience in the evangelical world over the past four decades has only caused this conviction to increase.

Mission and *evangelism* were virtually absent from much of the church's language by the time of the medieval church—an absence that left the church destitute of a strong kingdom theology for centuries. Even the Protestant Reformation, with all its emphasis on the gospel of justification by grace alone, did not fully rediscover this biblical emphasis. Darrell Guder observes, "Very few theologians, in the formal sense, took mission and evangelism seriously. The question of mission is not found in the major confessional documents of Western Christendom before the early twentieth century."[15]

When the modern missionary movement developed, it was primarily carried out by grassroots Christians and generally did not spring from a deeply developed theology that took the church seriously. Eventually the modern mission movement saw that theology was important. But this marriage has never been completely harmonious. Sadly, theology and mission have never been comfortable partners since the early centuries of Christianity. The fruit of this troubled marriage is increasingly significant. The problem is that most of our leaders do not understand why.

I believe the problem is clear: we have not trained our leaders to think and lead missionally. As a result, our leaders place little or no importance on unity in Christ's mission. Unity is even seen by many modern leaders as an obstacle to the more practical programs we employ to grow a church numerically. Who needs *other* Christians, *other* traditions, or *other* churches when you focus on your own programs and goals and build a growing (successful) church?

The discussion of evangelism tended, therefore, to stress the methods and practices of evangelism. As Guder noted, "All assumed that the Western missionary brought the correct understanding of the gospel to the nonbelieving culture and needed only to figure out how to convey it accurately and persuasively."[16]

The famous theologian Karl Barth gave a lecture in 1932 about the **missio Dei** (mission of God). Barth was likely the first theologian to see that mission was an aspect of God's nature. He saw mission as a movement from God to the world. The church was the instrument of God's mission. Simply put, there is a church *because* there is a mission. I suggest that our categories for mission are simply too small, just as our categories for the church are too small. The two go hand in hand. We must begin to teach leaders and churches to grasp "the comprehensive nature of God's mission."[17]

It is here that we discover the real problem. The temptation for churches, both those that are declining and those that are growing, is to focus on their own survival and growth. This cuts at the heart of the gospel by reducing ministry to numerical growth and explains why we have so many different gospel versions in free-market America. Indeed, if you do not like a particular American version of the gospel, you can attack someone else's gospel and then make up your own. Among evangelicals this has produced endless gospel wars accompanied by huge debates, conferences, and books. Darrell Guder has correctly observed that "reductionism does not mean that what remains is wrong; it means that what remains is too little—the church did not set aside the gospel; it reduced it and made it manageable."[18] This is a lot closer to the truth than modern evangelical gospel warriors realize.

When we reduce the gospel to manageable ideas, we demonize other Christians who do not preach the gospel as we do. A favorite text can be Galatians 1:6 – 9, where Paul warns about false gospels. (Rarely do those who use this text pay careful attention to the context or its social setting; instead it becomes another proof text for attacking Christians!)

For some years I engaged in these endless attempts to explain the true gospel. I was quite sure I was a faithful defender of the great truths of the Protestant Reformation. The bad guys were the Roman Catholics. Sometimes I even raised polemical questions about the Methodists and Pentecostals. I sincerely believed I was defending the faith. Now, looking back over several decades of involvement in these attempts to reform the church, I believe my efforts lacked both clarity and charity. Sadly, I helped to divide Christians. I pursued reductionism and made other Christians the enemy.

My approach was not totally wrong. Most of the things we attempt are never totally wrong. People in this present culture do play fast and loose with truth. Without truth there is no real Christianity. (Think back to chapter 10, where we saw that truth is not found in a system that arranges doctrines in logical formulas.) This is especially true where false gospels are distributed through pop culture and fads. But I am now firmly convinced that without a serious commitment to missional-ecumenism, we will never get the proper balance needed for modern reformation.

WE MUST LOVE ONE ANOTHER FIRST

I met Brother Yun, the Chinese Christian whose story is told in *The Heavenly Man*, in the fall of 2008. In some ways this amazing man has taught me as much about Christian unity as anyone I've ever met. Brother Yun believes the solution to division lies in rediscovering our true home in the love of Jesus through his commission to disciple all the nations, which is precisely my thesis if you have followed my thinking to this point. Brother Yun writes:

> Most of our church disputes and petty infighting come when we start arguing about unimportant matters. Our eyes come off the Great Commission and we start to fight one another instead of fighting against the works of the Devil, which is the very reason Jesus Christ came into the world. The Bible plainly declares, "The reason the Son of God appeared was to destroy the devil's work" (1 John 3:8).[19]

Jesus put it simply: "By this everyone will know you are my disciples, if you love one another" (John 13:35). Thus the prayer of Jesus in John 17 indicates that divisions are "natural" to this life but the unity Jesus prayed for is "supernatural."[20] True spiritual unity is meant to confound the wicked and attract the lost. Simply put, we are to love *all* people. But John 13:35 states we are to love our fellow Christians first. The apostle Paul agrees when he writes, "As we have opportunity, let us do good to all people, especially to those who belong to the family of believers" (Galatians 6:10). As counterintuitive as it seems, we love the world best when we love one another first. It seems that if our love for one another is real, it cannot help but impact the world.

QUESTIONS FOR DISCUSSION AND REFLECTION

1. How would you define the concept of the missional church in your own words? How does the use of this term change the way most of us have been taught to think about missions?

2. How can a church begin to think of itself as the missional people of God and then act like this kind of community in its life and witness? Be specific in your response.

3. If mission is part of the very nature of God, what are the implications for everything the church does? Have we reduced the nature of God to programs and activities rather than to being his people in mission?

chapter seventeen

A New Paradigm

Any concern for fresh spiritual life that is in accordance with the teaching of the New Testament must also lead to a concern for the unity of the church. Our search is not for uniformity. But it is only when we can pray together, work together, worship together, break bread together, and truly love and trust one another, that we can begin to speak of a united church, however varied its form of expression and worship may continue to be.

David Watson

WE HAVE DISCOVERED THAT *UNITY* is a beautiful word, a powerful ideal, and a clear biblical truth. The psalmist concludes, "How good and pleasant it is when God's people live together in unity" (133:1). The picture portrayed by this psalm is one of shared worship within a family of godly, refreshed, and consecrated people who walk in the abundance of God's divine presence. God always desires this unity for his people. The entire biblical record bears witness to this truth.

Sadly, there has been a great deal of confusion about unity for hundreds of years. On one side, many believe that any serious consideration of Christian unity will lead to compromise; on the other side, many believe that giving serious attention to doctrinal teaching will hinder serious efforts for unity. I have learned that the struggle between the practice of unity and the importance of biblical doctrine creates tension.

I have also come to realize that this tension has to be prayerfully engaged because solitary Christianity is dangerous and irresponsible. I use the word *tension* because of the mental and emotional strain we experience when we are faced with deep realities that make us uncomfortable—a tension that is the result of two truths we sense are pulling against each other.

THE TWO EXTREMES

Many Christians have dealt with this tension by placing the perspective they reject into a locked box and stuffing it far, far away. A broad-based call for the reunion of churches "at any cost" has misled and frightened some. Relativism, with a denial of essential Christian orthodoxy, has brought about what one author has provocatively called "the death of Protestant America."[1]

In broad-based calls for ecumenism rooted in the shared opinions of ecclesiastical executives and certain social classes, the gospel has sometimes been tragically lost. Respect for the ancient confessions and standards of the early church have all but collapsed. Churches become weak when they acknowledge only a vaguely defined catholicity that is not anchored in deep faith.

On the other side of this tension are many of the most vibrant Christians I have ever known. They hold a very high view of the Scripture but often have little passion for Christian unity. These Christians may even choose to treat unity as the enemy of the gospel. In my tradition, efforts for unity were seen as ultimately harmful to the task of protecting the pure gospel. At best, efforts for unity with people not like us were a waste of precious time—time that could have been better invested in reaching non-Christians.

On the side where I lived my faith for decades, we rarely dealt with the implications of the central passages of Scripture considered in this book—for example, John 17 and Ephesians 4. As a result, we remained in our sectarian mind-set. We reasoned that most of those who were unlike us were probably liberal. To be conservative was to be faithful; to be liberal was to deny Christ. We defended Scripture and engaged in numerous battles about the way to understand the Bible. In time, these battles became central to our identity.

The problem was that the more we focused on our commitment to the Bible, the more we drew dark lines of distinction ("us" and "them"). We even developed groups and movements in which we could defend our position against other conservative Christians not on our team. Our obvious tribalism may very well become our undoing in the upcoming decades if we do not adopt a new paradigm, a more biblical pattern for church life.

RECONCILIATION

My goal has been to show you that both extremes are unhealthy and that all three of the great Christian traditions—Catholic, Protestant, and Orthodox—have a serious contribution to make to each other. I have personally witnessed the truth that the most powerful evidence we have that division can be transcended is seen in the total giving of oneself for the sake of the gospel.[2] This is why I believe missional-ecumenism can so powerfully impact the twenty-first century.

I believe the three great divisions within historic Christianity were never desirable and quite likely were not truly necessary. But regardless of how these divisions came about, we can begin a healthy new conversation, a conversation that can lead to reconciliation in a context where the truth is profoundly important. This conversation could well become one of the Holy Spirit's primary ways of pushing forward the "new ecumenism"—an ecumenism rooted in core orthodoxy and deeply shared love for Christ and his mission. Vatican II's decree on ecumenism (*Unitatis Redintegratio*) called this "spiritual ecumenism" and believed it should be regarded as the true soul of the ecumenical movement.[3]

JAMES I. PACKER: MY TEACHER

One of the most significant persons in my personal journey has been Dr. James I. Packer, who helped me understand ecumenism in a way that led me to struggle with the two great truths I have mentioned. He has taught and lived "spiritual ecumenism" for a lifetime. He gave me more by his gracious spirit and generous orthodoxy than by powerful arguments, though he has made good arguments about Christian unity. By engaging in the dialogue of ecumenism from within an evangelical and biblical context, Packer helped me view apostolic tradition with fresh eyes and a genuinely open heart.

Dr. Packer rightly concludes that Jesus never had in mind an "all-embracing ecclesiastical organization" in his prayer in John 17.[4] But Packer also states that when we share together in relational oneness, the Spirit will guide us to "see eye to eye with each other regarding God's nature, will, and work, so that a shared orthodoxy ["right belief," as the word literally means] will take form and be firmly held among them."[5] I have witnessed this firsthand for more than a decade. This is the place to pursue missional-ecumenism. This approach has the advantage of not opposing formal ecumenical dialogue while at the same time putting the stress where Jesus placed it—on our personal relationships with other Christians and congregations.

Packer adds that this call to Christian unity will include "togetherness of spiritual life: togetherness that is in what Jesus called 'eternal life' and in a meditative moment in his prayer defined as knowing 'you the only true God, and Jesus Christ'—me!—'whom you sent' (John 17:3)." He then goes on to explain four implications:

- recognizing the reality of God and the Lord Jesus Christ
- responding to the impact of the Father and the Son mediated through the apostolic word, just as living things in this world respond to physical stimulation
- the inner change that Jesus described to Nicodemus as being born again of water and the Spirit (John 3:3–7), whereby Jesus dying for sins and drawing us to himself becomes the central focus of our life (3:14–21)
- the imparting by God of energy to stand against the world and the Devil and to spread the gospel message (17:14–16, 20)

Packer sums it up in this way: "This supernatural Christlikeness results from Christ himself being in us, united to each one in a way that sustains the divine life in the human soul and binds us all to each other through the binding of each one to the other."[6]

Dr. Packer's understanding of unity includes "a togetherness of active love: love that is motivated and animated by knowledge of the redemptive, life-transforming love of God to us (John 17:23, 26)." Such an active love will work diligently, in the spirit of gospel reconciliation, to honor and exalt *everyone* who loves the Lord Jesus Christ. And because this is *holy* love, it will always be one that is "maintaining God's moral standards in all that it does."[7] The good sense of Dr. Packer's argument is so obvious that only those who have constructed a theological box will miss it.

Packer further affirms the correct note when he says that this togetherness should be centered in missional ministry. Read his comment carefully: "When the incarnate Son was on earth, the Father and he, the sender and the sent, were, as we would put it nowadays, on mission together.... The Son's post-resurrection commissioning of his disciples ... involves all Christians in the mission, one way or another." Packer concludes his consideration of the marks of our togetherness by adding, "We are called to be one, united and cooperating, in actively spreading the gospel, in and under Christ as mission leader."[8]

But what about the sacraments, orders for gospel ministry, church forms, and ecclesial organizations? Packer, an evangelical Anglican priest, sees belief in an apostolic succession through bishops as theologically and historically commendable, but he correctly concludes, "We [must] note that no form of church organization is mentioned, and we infer that organization will only be relevant to Christian unity insofar as it expresses and furthers the ones in Christ that we have described."[9] In my opinion, Dr. Packer's greatest strength is his ecumenism joined with his commitment to evangelical Christianity. Furthermore, this perspective lines up with Pope John XXIII's conviction that "what unites us is much greater than what divides us."[10]

These are the conclusions I have drawn as I have wrestled with this subject for the past fifteen years. I am fully supportive of every attempt to express true Christian unity in formal ways. We must continue to find new ways to foster the spirit of the ecumenical progress begun by John R. Mott and Lesslie Newbigin. These men demonstrate that the ecumenical movement had a good beginning and remind us that true ecumenism must always be rooted in mission, holiness, and prayer.

But as important as formal efforts for unity have been, the primary progress is still to be made in the trenches of shared life — person to person, school to school, congregation to congregation, movement to movement, and, sometimes, denomination to denomination. Real progress is being made in human relationships, within families and communities, in our cities and towns. This is where I believe the great principle of Christ the center, the same principle we saw in chapter 6, will show itself once again. This principle has been displayed in various movements for renewal that have taken place in all three of the great Christian churches. The renewal of the Holy Spirit brings about healthy ecumenism, at least until we begin to revert to the old sinful patterns that quench it. True revivals have always broken down barriers as awakened believers realize that they share in the same outpoured Spirit.

A DIFFERENT ANSWER

Some believe that the American church, at least as we have known it, is dying. I think these dismal conclusions miss what is happening at the grassroots level — in the places where Christians work and worship. I see the Holy Spirit stirring the church to rediscover the ancient paths of paleo-orthodoxy and to find new ways of living faithfully in a world no longer influenced by Christendom. I see a movement of bold, united prayer. I find men and women learning to practice the disciplines of ancient spiritual formation. I see a growing movement of convergence that seeks to recover the unity of God's people by learning from each other through shared involvement in the mission of Christ. This is all part of what I call missional-ecumenism.

I see at least seven common elements powerfully converging, with each stream indicating ways in which newer churches are learning from ancient churches, and vice versa. This informal ecumenism is creating a new life-giving river of grace as these streams converge to form a new expression of Christ's community in our time:

- *a restored commitment to the sacraments*, especially to regular celebrations at the Lord's Table. Neither the charismatic nor evangelical streams of Christianity have stressed this commitment, but evidence abounds that this is changing.

- *an increased appetite to know more about the early church.* For many Christians there has been a huge gap between the pages of their Bible and the modern church. The search for common roots has brought them to a deeper interest in the Catholic and Orthodox church.
- *an obvious open expression of love for the whole church and a real desire to see the church become one.* This growing regard for catholicity is more evident now than at any time in my six decades of life. Prayer for unity drives this expression, but conferences, seminars, retreats, and shared witnessing experiences fuel it.
- *the blending of the practices of worship, devotion, and prayer from all three streams,* even as churches approach this convergence from different emphases. Most congregations clearly reveal a particular expression of the church that regulates their life together. What is changing is that the convergence of several streams is drawing churches together while they retain their distinctive base. At the same time they are opening themselves up to the strengths of other churches they never knew.
- *an interest in integrating more liturgical depth and structure with spontaneity and freedom in the Holy Spirit.* Charismatic Christians are finding exciting treasures in liturgy, and liturgical Christians are finding deep joy in praise and the new song.
- *a greater involvement of sign and symbol in worship through banners, crosses, Christian art, and clerical vestments.* Some in the evangelical and charismatic movements are skeptical about these streams, but this movement that does not involve one stream as much as a convergence of several wonderful streams can only help each church to mature.
- *a continuing commitment to personal salvation, solid biblical teaching, and the work and ministry of the Holy Spirit.* The rich and vital heritage of the Protestant Reformation is not being abandoned but is being accessed in unheard-of ways as thousands of convergence-model Christians and

churches embrace these key elements of vital biblical Christianity.

In an increasingly postmodern context, these converging streams are creating what appear to be genuinely new wine-skins—wineskins into which God may pour new wine. We can no longer appeal to a Protestant America or even to a Catholic America, though there are now more Catholics than Protestants in America. We can't even refer to a "Christian America." The idea of saving our culture by restoring Christian America has plainly failed.

Younger Christians rightly see something better emerging on the horizon. What seems so odd to older Christians is that at the same time that the church has less direct influence on the culture, we see the Holy Spirit restoring the oneness of the church through deep relationships. Various streams of the church are converging into new movements of divine grace and mercy led by the small platoons of believers who deeply love Christ and his mission. They long to share their journey with all Christians. Could this movement of spiritual reconciliation be evidence that God is doing something powerful in our century and better things are yet to come? I believe so!

CONCLUSION

Although I still have misgivings about parts of the ecumenical movement—World Council of Churches, Vatican Council II, various evangelical alliances around the globe, and the charismatic movement—all of these have collectively helped us move toward a stronger experience of reconciliation. Think back to more than a century ago, and you discover we have made huge strides in Christian unity in almost every visible expression of the church except among the radical separatists. What we have often lacked in our judgments is an informed perspective, and in this book I have tried to give you such a perspective.

The late David Watson wrote these words three decades ago: "Among many Christian leaders there is the deep conviction that it is only by concentrating on the fundamentals of our faith, supremely the cross of Christ and the renewal of the Holy Spirit, that any real experience of unity will be a serious possibility."[11]

I have no doubt that Vatican II has had the most dramatic impact by opening the windows of the largest fellowship of Christians in the world to the fresh winds of the Holy Spirit. Vatican II's Dogmatic Constitution on the Church (*Lumen Gentium* 12) states,

> It is not only through the sacraments and the ministries of the church that the Holy Spirit sanctifies and leads the people of God and enriches it with virtues.... He distributes special graces among the faithful of every rank. By these gifts he makes them fit and ready to undertake various tasks and offices which contribute toward the renewal and building up of the church.[12]

This movement of the Holy Spirit was given major support by Léon Joseph Cardinal Suenens (1904–1996), one of the four moderators of the Vatican II. (Some believe he was used in a powerful way to keep the council from breaking down at critical junctures.) Cardinal Suenens once said, in response to a question about reconciliation between the churches, "I believe that the solution of ecumenical disunity will not finally be the result of a dialogue between the Church of Rome and the Church of Canterbury or the Church of Moscow. It will not be a dialogue between the churches as such, but a dialogue between Rome and Jesus, Canterbury and Jesus, Moscow and Jesus, so that we can become more and more united in him."[13] Happy is the one who sees the centrality of Jesus, explores the depth of what this truly means, and does this in deep relational fellowship with other Christ-centered Christians.

David Watson helped me picture how this reconciliation may advance when he suggested that when we travel by air and first lift off the ground, the walls, hedges, and buildings all look very large to us. The higher we rise, the smaller they become. In the same way, "When the power of the Holy Spirit lifts us up together into the conscious realization of the presence of Jesus, the barriers between us become unimportant. Seated with Christ in the heavenly places, the difference between Christians can often seem petty and marginal."[14]

As Jesus renews our hearts, we can begin to embrace a new paradigm that we had never dreamed possible until we took our place with Christ in heavenly places. I believe this new paradigm is rooted in the theology and practice of missional-ecumenism. I also believe it will deeply change your life and your church if you pursue it with me.

QUESTIONS FOR DISCUSSION AND REFLECTION

1. How do you understand the two extremes we face in dealing with ecumenism if you agree with the missional-ecumenism thesis? How do you propose to address these tensions in your church or mission while respecting the conscience of those who do not agree? How can you be a true peacemaker?

2. Do you believe that America is increasingly post-Christian? Why or why not? How should the church respond to the loss of our culture and the privileged place we once enjoyed? What does this loss mean for your mission?

3. How would you explain the term *ecumenical theology*? How could a theology of ecumenism be produced? Is it desirable to do so? Do you see any evidence it might happen?

chapter eighteen

What Does the Missional-Ecumenical Paradigm Look Like?

The church exists for mission as fire exists for burning.
Emil Brunner

One reason the church is failing today is that it has so many members who are not kingdom-of-God men and women! They may be active in the church program—regular at worship, involved in the administration of the religious establishment—but they lack kingdom-of-God qualities.
Richard Halverson

AS I HAVE WITNESSED a growing movement of the Holy Spirit bringing Christians together in relational unity I have also had the joy of hearing many stories that demonstrate the missional-ecumenical paradigm. These stories have encouraged me. I hope they will give you a glimpse into the practical outworking of missional-ecumenism.

What does the vision I have articulated look like in a specific city, region, or mission? How does a pastor or a city-impact mission leader help others pursue the kingdom of God through missional-ecumenism? The following stories are intended to answer these questions. I would love to hear your story if you are on the same road. Let me know what you've seen in your city or congregation. Perhaps sharing our stories will help us catch the fresh wind of God in our sails.[1]

THREE SPHERES OF INCARNATIONAL COMMUNITY

The one element that stands out powerfully in each of these stories is how the kingdom of God becomes tangible through incarnation. This happens when churches and ministries understand that mission is incarnational. Hugh Halter and Matt Smay express this truth in a concrete way in their important book *The Tangible Kingdom*.[2] Halter and Smay argue that the modern missional shift is not being led by wild-eyed radicals but by solidly orthodox Christians who are asking the questions that our era requires of faithful Christian leaders. These authors help us see more clearly how the kingdom intersects with our present context.

As you read these stories, you will be introduced to what Halter and Smay call "the tangible kingdom." Each story reveals a Christian person or a ministry that experienced the kingdom of God breaking into the life of the church or the work of several churches together. I am convinced that the kingdom of God becomes tangible when three spheres of reality—mission, communion, and community—come together. This tangible point of convergence is where the kingdom is made known.

Perhaps the most impressive thing I have discovered in my own journey is that the incarnational approach will produce an entirely different type of evangelism than the one in which I engaged in the 1970s and 1980s (an attractional approach). In this new paradigm, people are being invited to belong to a people before they are invited to believe a message. They are included rather than excluded.

If this paradigm is legitimate, then pastors and churches will have to think about how to alter the way they teach and practice evangelism. I am persuaded that putting this understanding into practice will take both great skill and deep spiritual formation.[3]

We dare not try to be missional-ecumenical unless we are empowered by the Holy Spirit. To employ the incarnational approach is hard work and requires us to die if we are to live in the reality of the kingdom.

How can we understand the difference between *attractional* evangelism and *incarnational* evangelism. I find the following diagram helpful.

COMPARISON OF ATTRACTIONAL AND INCARNATIONAL APPROACHES

Attractional Approach	Incarnational Approach
Unbeliever is invited to church	Sojourner is invited to belong
Unbeliever confesses belief	Sojourner confesses interest
Unbeliever repeats a prayer	Sojourner experiences the good news
Believer joins church	Sojourner participates in community
Cognitive discipleship	Experiential apprenticeship
Focus: counting confessions	Focus: transformation
Believing enables belonging	Belonging enables believing

Figure 18.1: Taken from Hugh Halter and Matt Smay, *The Tangible Kingdom: Creating Incarnational Community* (San Francisco: Jossey-Bass, 2008), 95. Used by permission.

What does incarnational evangelism look like? Let's listen to some stories. Many people and churches are practicing missional theology, whether they realize it or not. And many of these people and churches are pursuing unity with other churches and Christians as well. These stories are meant to give you pictures that will encourage you to pursue missional-ecumenism.

A NEW CHURCH PLANT WITH A DIFFERENT VISION

No one whom I have ever taught and mentored brings me more joy than my son, Matthew John Armstrong. Several years ago, Matt became, in his own words, an "accidental church planter." He began a ministry in Streamwood, Illinois, that is committed to reaching middle school young people in a racially and ethnically diverse community through after-school clubs in public schools. The fruitfulness of this mission and his commitment to the church compelled him to plant New Hope Community in 2007.

Matt envisioned a missional and ecumenical church from the start. He wanted to reach people and grow a church, but he also wanted to serve the kingdom in his community. His church (New Hope) formed an initial core of people and then began public worship. They did the usual marketing stuff—ads, door hangers, invitations to events and festivals and the like. But they also aimed to transform their community by working with other Christians and churches. Because of this commitment Matt reached out to local ministers. He assured them that his goal was to help reach the 85 percent of the people in their town who did not attend church. He had an experience in which God spoke these words to his heart: "I have given you Streamwood, but you must work for unity."

So Matt and his church set out to understand their community. They invited pastors to a luncheon. It was a flop! He didn't give up. He met with a local minister from a church that most evangelicals would consider "too liberal." (They met through the local Kiwanis Club; Matt's involvement there was another part of his kingdom strategy.) He tried a second ministers meeting, this time with his new friend's help. Only the two of them showed up. Then he tried to get personal phone numbers and email addresses for each pastor. He met with more difficulty. He found pastors impossibly busy and hard to reach. But he was determined because of his vision for Christ's kingdom.

After prayer and fasting it was back to the drawing board. Matt scheduled one-on-one meetings with the leaders of Lutheran, Baptist, Catholic, and independent churches. Soon he decided to cancel his Sunday morning service and send people out in small groups to visit the churches of Streamwood. His folks handed the leaders a copy of a DVD called "Transformations." They hand-delivered a letter from Matt asking how New Hope could pray for their church.

After more prayer and more failure, the seed began to take root. There were nine churches in Matt's community. Before the end of 2008, seven of these nine churches (plus one from outside the community) were involved in a meaningful relationship with each other. In the summer of 2008, the local Roman Catholic parish gave a gift to Matt's congregation to support a mission project in Latin America. (Read that sentence again if you wonder about what is happening in local communities.) In the fall, people from the seven churches participated in a prayer walk.[4] (The two churches that would not participate were separatist congregations.)

AN ESTABLISHED EVANGELICAL CHURCH GETS A NEW MISSION

For many years I have personally related to a church in a nearby community. I have known the last two pastors well. When the current pastor and I visited in the summer of 2008, I discovered he had gone through a lot of personal change, and his church had shifted a bit as well. As a result, this church has partnered with other congregations, even helping one church replant in a nearby suburb.

As I listened, my friend shared an intriguing story. He said God had been working for years to impress on him that his message was for the whole body of Christ. This pastor began to ask how he could make a corporate application of every sermon. He asked, "What is God saying to *us*? What does obedience look like for *us*?" Then he dared to ask, "What does this word mean for the greater church and the world?" Soon he found himself in Ephesians 4 and 5, discovering that Ephesians 5 puts the church in the context of a relational family. What he feared was "political correctness"; what he discovered was unity in the Godhead. Through this he discovered the powerful connection between his church and the kingdom of God. As a result, his church became an intentional sending and planting center for other kingdom-centered churches.

In 1990, the previous pastor had prayed that God would send ten people out into mission. (This is not a large church.) It wasn't until 1995 that the first person was sent — the pastor himself. (This is almost identical to my own story.) From 1996 to 2008, this church sent forty-three more people into mission (for two or more years of service). The parent church is now smaller — which causes some to believe that the strategy failed. I beg to differ. I can't think of a more successful pastor or church in my area.

This pastor recently wrote me an email that stated, "We're smaller in number (by far) than we've ever been, sometimes depressingly so. Part of our decline is due to sending out our brightest and best. Part of it is due to mistakes I've made in ministry. I think (at least I hope) I've finally learned that I can't please everybody. When I try to do that, I frustrate everybody." He concluded his email by writing, "We're making a worldwide impact through the people whom we have on the mission field and through church planting. But I'm praying that the people of our church will catch a second wind for impacting our community. I'd appreciate your prayers to that end." Indeed, I am praying for that!

MAINLINE CHURCHES GET A VISION

A Lutheran pastor who serves on the ACT 3 board was called to his first church in a rural county seat town in Ohio in the early 1990s. The community faced high unemployment rates and contained mostly small, struggling churches, with only two large congregations in the area. Most of the ministers were in their first or second call and knew they would probably stay at their churches for only three or four years. And most of the churches had no denominational neighbors in the county. There was, however, a long history of a functioning ministerial group. (Interestingly, this group traced its roots back to the days of prohibition when a Catholic priest and a Reformed minister got together to brew their own beer.)

During my friend's pastorate, these ministers engaged in a lot of discussion, but very little in the way of a missional-ecumenical nature was ever done. It then dawned on these pastors that they should join together to sponsor a Vacation Bible School—with a goal of overcoming disagreements about dates and curriculum. Seven congregations, none of which had restrictions about praying and worshiping together, rented a local elementary school and did VBS for the community. The churches were Lutheran, United Church of Christ, Methodist, Baptist, African Methodist Episcopal, and Presbyterian. My friend writes, "We hosted five hundred-plus kids, and the world didn't end. If anything, the kingdom of God happened in our midst."

This same pastor then moved on to another rural Ohio congregation, where similar things happened in a different form. In this community, there were two Lutheran churches (one that had to be careful about ecumenism because of denominational barriers), a Southern Baptist church, a Methodist church, and a Church of God church. The ministers met, drank coffee, and prayed. They began to pursue ways in which they could serve Christ's kingdom together.

In this instance, they not only shared a VBS; they also bought supplies in bulk to lower the price for their members. They had fund-raisers for building projects and for people in need. They spontaneously showed up at one another's buildings with food to be shared at social events. One pastor was reported to his denominational leader by a young seminarian and had to curtail some of his involvement. The group adjusted and worked hard to keep him involved in every way possible. The glue that kept these ministers together was their love for Christ, for each other, and for the people in their struggling town. They were missional-ecumenical pastors.

AN INTERRACIAL MISSION IN ONE OF AMERICA'S POOREST COUNTIES

In 1988, Tunica County in Mississippi was listed as the poorest county in America. Most of the black families who lived there two decades ago were below the poverty level. The county was well known for racial segregation. Enter Dr. Paul Husband, an Evangelical Presbyterian Church minister whose deep desire was to see God at work in reconciliation. Paul understood that the cross breaks down walls of separation and creates unity. He decided to address racial reconciliation in his own congregation and then in the county.

When Paul came to Tunica in 1988, he thought he would get to know several black pastors so he could share what he had learned in seminary. But the pastors were so busy working secular jobs forty to fifty hours a week and preaching on Sundays that they didn't have time for Paul's tutelage. He notes, after many years, "It's a good thing they didn't!"

Then the situation began to change. Paul writes:

> In the spring of 1996, black pastor Rodney Hibbler invited
> me to attend the youth group he and his wife, Jenny, led on
> Tuesday evenings. Rodney had only a high school education
> and no seminary training. I thought I would be able to help
> him with his youth group since I had been a youth minister
> for seven years and had both an MDiv degree and a PhD in
> church history. Was I ever wrong!
>
> When I arrived that night, about 120 teenagers were
> packed into a small church singing praise and worship
> songs with all their might. Rodney next opened the floor
> for one-sentence testimonies. One by one, the teenagers
> stood and gave praise to God: "I just thank God for the
> privilege of singing his praise tonight." "I praise God for
> the Bible." "I praise my Lord Jesus for changing my heart
> and forgiving me all my sins." Everyone had something for
> which they gave thanks and praise to the Lord. Next the
> Bible study began, and the teenagers participated by quot-
> ing Bible verse after Bible verse with Rodney and Jenny.
> I had planned on helping them do youth ministry—even
> though I had a hard time getting fifteen teenagers to attend
> my youth group, much less sing praises with gusto, give
> testimonies, and quote Scripture. God humbled me that
> night and showed me how much I could learn from my black
> brothers and sisters.

The Lord knit the hearts of Paul and Rodney together as they
grew to trust each other in a relationship of mutual love and
respect. Paul soon learned that Rodney knew his Bible backward
and forward and could preach circles around him. Paul felt led
to invite Rodney, his son, and his brother to attend a Promise
Keepers rally in Memphis in the fall of 1996. As they continued to
fellowship and pray together, they began to believe that the Lord
was calling them to draw together black and white pastors alike
in Tunica County to fulfill the Great Commission. The result was
a Ministers Association comprised of five black pastors and four
white pastors. They met each week in Paul's home to study Henry
Blackaby's book *Experiencing God*. Out of that study, these nine
pastors began a mutual outreach effort, agreeing to bring short-
term missions to Tunica.

Rodney and Paul invited Adventures in Mission (AIM), Southern Baptists, several Christian colleges, and Paul's own denomination, the Evangelical Presbyterian Church (EPC), to join in short-term missions and help facilitate racial reconciliation. Over the past twelve years, these groups and pastors have joined forces to host over 5,500 short-term missionaries who have come to Tunica County to pray and work for Christ's kingdom.

Their activity has consisted of repairing and painting homes, reroofing churches, conducting Vacation Bible Schools and basketball camps, operating health clinics, engaging in a nursing home ministry, doing sports evangelism and door-to-door evangelism, sponsoring prayer ministries, and participating in local jail missions. The churches have placed New Testaments and gospel tracts in over 2,500 homes. Paul reports that "our gracious Lord has allowed us to see over 4,000 professions of faith in Christ as a result of the mission here in Tunica County. We now have plans to expand to other small Mississippi delta towns."

This is missional-ecumenism at its best. In an out-of-the-way place many of us would not see as important to the future of Christianity in America, God clearly had other ideas. I am sure that God sees this as a movement of "big" churches who understand the kingdom of God.

REACHING PEOPLE OF THE NIGHT: CATHOLICS AND EVANGELICALS IN THE STREETS OF CHICAGO

One of the more amazing missional-ecumenical stories I have had the joy of being a part of personally is being lived out on the north side of Chicago. Emmaus Ministries (*www.streets.org*) was founded by John Green, a permanent deacon in the Roman Catholic archdiocese of Chicago. John, a cradle Catholic and fervent evangelical, earned two academic degrees at Wheaton College. His vision is to evangelize and transform the streets of a Chicago neighborhood where homosexual prostitution is a major part of the culture. His efforts have been blessed with amazing fruitfulness. His missional partners include Catholics and Protestants.

By focusing on the mission of Christ and keeping the church at the center of his vision, John has done what few have been able to accomplish—incarnating the love of Christ on the streets and introducing the kingdom of God into one of the darkest corners of a large city. Not only has John, with his staff and volunteers, extended the gospel into many broken lives; he has done it by cooperating with evangelical schools and churches and Roman Catholic congregations. His work involves priests, laypeople, and parish councils. Throughout the week, a person who visits Emmaus will see folks from various Christian traditions working side by side as they share the love of Christ. It results in a glorious mosaic and is one of the best displays of missional-ecumenism I know of.

ALPHA: A COURSE THAT CHANGES LIVES

Perhaps no single church-based mission has touched more Catholics and Protestants together than the internationally known Alpha course—a ten-week course in which the implications of Christianity are explored in a relaxed and thought-provoking atmosphere. Alpha courses have been taught in churches, prisons, universities, and military bases. This mission began at Holy Trinity Church (Brompton, England), an Anglican charismatic parish. The goal of the course is to explore the meaning of life in a stress-free, relational atmosphere.

Alpha has spread from England to the world. Participants have included bishops and archbishops from North America, Africa, and Asia—and even the head of the Coptic Church in North Africa. One Middle Eastern delegate to a recent Alpha gathering said, "We are seeing history in the making here. Not for many centuries have Christians of every denomination come together around one piece of Christian teaching in this way." I wholeheartedly agree. Whenever I meet a mainline Protestant congregation alive with the Spirit and seeing people come to faith as a part of their regular ministry, I almost always discover that Alpha is there. Over eleven million people worldwide have attended an Alpha course. Now several Alpha look-alike courses are springing up in other contexts.

PRAYER MOVEMENTS: THE POWER NEEDED FOR EFFECTIVE MISSIONAL-ECUMENISM

There are so many prayer movements spanning the globe that it is hard to keep up with this phenomenon. One such movement I have had firsthand exposure to is the Church Prayer Leaders Network, led by Jonathan Graf. There is even a Global Day of Prayer that spans the planet and gathers Christians to pray for spiritual awakening! The North American leader of this ministry is another friend, Robert Bakke. Bob is a missional-ecumenical leader who longs to see a global awakening that will bring Christians together to complete Christ's mission. In the Chicago area, my good friend Phil Miglioratti leads several prayer ministries that touch the lives of hundreds of churches and leaders. His prayer card "30 Days of Prayer for Our Cities" is one of the best tools I have seen for teaching people how to engage in specific kingdom prayer for their city.

These prayer movements have touched issues such as racial reconciliation, community development, pastor's prayer networks, and various forms of servant evangelism. Though much of this movement is evangelical, there are growing numbers of Catholics sharing in prayer for worldwide spiritual awakening. I see this as a fire that has been burning for two decades and pray that a massive conflagration may soon break out as the Holy Spirit meets with prayer leaders from all across the world. Most of America's major cities have a significant ministry of prayer, even though many residents do not know it exists.

Pope John Paul II urged Christians to "grow ever more in united common prayer around Christ" so they can pursue the ecumenism God is directing. He wrote, "If they meet more often and more regularly before Christ in prayer, they will be able to gain the courage to face all the painful human reality of their divisions." The pope added, "It is true that we are not yet in full communion. And yet, despite our divisions, we are on the way toward full unity, that unity which marked the apostolic church at its birth and which we sincerely seek. Our common prayer, inspired by faith, is proof of this."[5] This desire is being met by a growing missional-ecumenical response all across America.

MISSIONAL-ECUMENISM FLOURISHES WHERE CHRISTENDOM ONCE REIGNED

The United Kingdom has experienced a serious decline in church attendance over the past one hundred years. In many places, less than 2 to 3 percent of the population attends church. The strongest Christian presence is evangelical, and members of these churches have nurtured spiritual life in the whole church.

Dr. Michael Quicke, professor of homiletics at Northern Baptist Theological Seminary, served for many years as a Baptist pastor and respected evangelical leader in the United Kingdom. He relates that in Britain's secularized context a new kind of ecumenism has been spreading over the last decades—an informal and missional ecumenism that is spawning large and small events across the nation.

One huge annual event is Spring Harvest, with sixty to seventy thousand Christians (both young and old) gathering each year, drawn from many different churches and denominational backgrounds, including house churches, charismatic churches, and liturgical churches. Michael has spoken at this event and says many workshops are led by two or three teachers who work together. Attendees of workshop sessions do not know in advance who the speakers will be. Michael has found himself working alongside charismatic Anglicans, female Salvation Army officers, a Pentecostal house church leader, and an overseas Methodist missionary. The number of different leaders and groups are too numerous to list. He writes, "I found the level of sharing and the assumptions by the organizers that we would work together a staggering example of evangelicals sharing together."

Michael also served a Baptist church in historic Cambridge. In the 1990s, he also chaired the Cambridge Christian Festival. A large tent was set up in the main public commons in the town, and an evangelistic speaker preached each night. The organizing committee represented churches from across the entire spectrum. Over two hundred congregations participated. The group made plain that evangelism, no holds barred, was the purpose of the festival. Every denominational group was involved, including Roman Catholics. Those who resisted did so for two reasons: the evangelistic emphasis was a turnoff to them (liberal churches), or the collaboration was too broad (fundamentalist churches). The tent raised in the town had a massive banner at the top that read, "Jesus Is Our Lord."

TAIZÉ: A COMMUNITY WHERE MISSIONAL-ECUMENISM LIVES

The Taizé community is an ecumenical Christian monastic order located in a small place in Burgundy, France. Founded in 1940 by Frère Roger (Brother Roger), a Reformed Protestant minister, it was originally a sanctuary for World War II refugees. Both Catholics and Protestants have shared life and ministry together at Taizé for nearly seventy years. The intentional ecumenism of Taizé is experienced in prayers and music offered in many languages and chants and icons from the Eastern Orthodox tradition. Taizé has never wanted to be a movement but rather a place where young people could be encouraged at youth meetings and then sent back to their local churches and communities to pursue a "pilgrimage of trust on earth."[6] Many Americans know of Taizé because of the music it has spread around the globe.

A recent book by Jason Brian Santos, *A Community Called Taizé*, tells the story of this unique mission as a spiritual focal point for millions of young people throughout the world.[7] It is an order that attracts countless visitors from the whole church who take on the lifestyle of missional-ecumenism. Taizé stands as one of the most powerful ecumenical symbols in the world by living an incarnational model of peace and reconciliation. Here popes and evangelicals have drawn strength in prayer and worship by sharing life together. When John Paul II died, Brother Roger was an honored participant in his funeral service, even receiving Mass from his dear friend Cardinal Joseph Ratzinger just days before Cardinal Ratzinger became Pope Benedict XVI.

MISSIONAL-ECUMENISM IN THE LARGER AMERICAN CONTEXT: *EVANGELICALS AND CATHOLICS TOGETHER*

No ecumenical endeavor has brought about as much interest among American evangelicals, at least over the past fifteen years, as Evangelicals and Catholics Together (ECT)—the fulfillment of the dream of Charles W. Colson and the late Father Richard John Neuhaus. I believe ECT has accomplished more for informal ecumenism and Christ's mission than we realize. While it prompted huge negative reactions from well-known evangelicals, in many ways it serves as a model of the very things I have written about.

My initial reaction to ECT was negative because I only saw it through the lens of the sixteenth-century theological debate. As time went on, I had to undergo one of the more painful changes in my life, as this movement compelled me to reexamine my attitudes and actions. I was eventually drawn into private meetings with several of the leading figures in this evangelical debate, where I had to learn to listen.

I remember asking Chuck Colson, "What did you want to accomplish with this ecumenical effort?" He calmly replied, "I want to see doors opened for Christ's mission, especially in Latin America." (The original idea, before ECT, was to convene a symposium to discuss the growing rivalry between Catholics and evangelicals in Latin America.) Colson said he wanted to preach Christ where he could not and to love all Christians. It may make no difference to his critics, but one fact is now abundantly clear: hundreds of prisons that were previously closed were opened to the witness of the gospel. I believe history will look on these developments with more favor than critics realize.[8]

My friend T. M. Moore has been involved in ECT from the beginning. He told me about how this process proceeded after the first document was issued. ECT created a storm that did not go away, but the committee kept meeting and writing, clarifying agreements and disagreements between Catholics and evangelicals. The entire process, though unofficial, is impressive in demonstrating how serious Catholics and serious evangelicals can accomplish so much by working together in the same room, bathed by the spirit of love and prayer.

Moore believes the contemporary church can achieve so much more in the way of vital, visible unity if we would learn to listen more humbly. He says the ECT process—which includes a twice-annual day for discussion, sharing, fellowship, prayer, and dialogue about issues that unite and divide Catholics and evangelicals—has been difficult and exhilarating. The participants struggle to come up with ways to say what it is they agree on but often cannot easily find the right words to express their conclusions. Sometimes people will open the Greek New Testament and carefully discuss various textual meanings and ideas in considerable depth. Each side will express themselves in ways that take the edge off of what would otherwise widen their differences. Remarkably, the group is often able to put aside the ways they would normally say something so they can achieve terminology that both sides will accept — and yet not have to compromise core beliefs.

In a private letter written in July 2008, Moore notes, "Differences surface from time to time, some of them quite serious, but so far none have been of the sort to cause concern about heresy or compromise, nor have any threatened to disrupt the spirit of fellowship, collaboration, and unity that is renewed and deepened with each subsequent meeting. The meetings and meals are salted with good humor, gracious forbearance, mutual respect, and gritty determination to find words to use in expressing our common convictions about core matters of the historic Christian faith."

Moore concludes that such forums could be created at the local level, where pastors and thoughtful laypeople from all communions could come together to discuss how to arrive at united positions on matters of pressing concern to their local churches and community. This is exactly what I have undertaken in Chicago. I believe these efforts will spread in the years to come.

QUESTIONS FOR DISCUSSION AND REFLECTION

1. As you reflect on the stories and models of missional-ecumenism found here, prayerfully ponder how these stories can inform your own story in your unique context. What kind of alliances and missional ventures would stir a vision for Christ's kingdom in your own community? In your own local congregation? In your Christian school or organization?

2. How can missional-ecumenical models be encouraged while you remain faithful to the doctrines your church/mission/school believes are nonnegotiable because of your particular history and calling? Where is the right place to begin pursuing this vision in terms of your leadership and service?

chapter nineteen

Disturb Us, Lord!

Disturb us, Lord, when we are too well pleased with ourselves, when our dreams have come true because we have dreamed too little, when we arrive safely because we sailed too close to the shore.

Disturb us, Lord, when with the abundance of things we possess we have lost our thirst for the waters of life; having fallen in love with life, we have ceased to dream of eternity; and in our efforts to build a new earth, we have allowed our vision of the new heaven to dim.

Disturb us, Lord, to dare more boldly, to venture on wider seas where storms will show your mastery; where losing sight of land, we shall find the stars. We ask you to push back the horizons of our hopes, and to push us into the future in strength, courage, hope, and love.

Attributed to Sir Francis Drake, 1577

I HAVE ALWAYS HAD A GREAT INTEREST in exploration. I used to disappear for hours, sometimes causing my mother grave concern. I would explore new places—wooded lots and even little caves. I especially liked to explore new books and old photographs, holed up in our attic for hours. I am not quite sure why, but I always had an insatiable desire to learn new things and discover new places. Perhaps this is why the greatest explorer of the Elizabethan Age, Sir Francis Drake (1540–1596), holds such a particular fascination for me. His explorations of the West Indies made him an amazing celebrity.

Drake was a devout Christian whose passion for exploration came from his deep faith. The prayer of this remarkable explorer (see the epigraph at this chapter's opening) makes a fitting conclusion for this exploration. I am sure I am not done exploring. There are new places to go and new people to meet. There is more to learn and much more to obey. I feel like I have only just begun.

"WHERE THERE ARE SINS, THERE ARE DIVISIONS"

The ancient church writer Origen (AD 185–254) studied under one of the first great postapostolic theologians, Clement of Alexandria (155–220). He became a famous lecturer and is still respected as a Greek father of the church. His theology is both praised and criticized. One of the most important things that Origen ever wrote about the church is found in this saying: *Ubi peccata sunt, ibi est multitudo*— "Where there are sins, there are divisions."[1] It should be apparent that I share his perspective.

Many Christians, especially evangelical Christians, have accepted the idea that a deeply divided church is normative. Some even believe mission is best advanced through this divided church. To challenge this mind-set is not easy, but I believe it is time for Christians to reconsider the ecumenical implications of believing that there is "one holy catholic and apostolic church."

The famous Reformer John Calvin said he would "cross ten seas" to further the unity of the church.[2] Would you cross the street? If you share my perspective, then you may have to cross troubled seas. I am sure you cannot do this unless you draw deeply from the whole Christian tradition, search the Scriptures with a renewed vision for the supremacy of Christ and his kingdom, and pray fervently for Christian unity. We must begin by calling individuals to personal responsibility before God. We must work to restore the essential truths of paleo-orthodox Christianity. This will require a fresh vision of the beauty and power of Christian tradition, core orthodoxy, and thoughtful catholicity. I am persuaded that nothing less than a gracious outpouring of the Holy Spirit will ultimately change us. We see this happening in China. Why not here?

THE SHADOWS OF CHRISTENDOM

For centuries, the church in America has ministered within a culture of Christendom, in a complex religious arrangement whereby

Christians generally had cultural and religious authority. This cultural form of faith is now passing away, for better or for worse. The church seems to have lost its way during the transition. Many churches have adapted to the culture in a way that has left them with little or no prophetic message. They have embraced a paradigm designed by Christendom and aimed at consumers—a paradigm that has left them with a shallow understanding of the gospel. Some who fervently believe in the need to remain faithful to the gospel have reacted to all the changes by accusing fellow Christian evangelists of being compromisers. Neither strategy is effective. We need a new paradigm, a model for mission that is rooted in antiquity and the dynamic prospects of a different future.

We should be asking a simple question: What is the real purpose of Christ's church in the world? This question will lead us to see that the world we live in is more like the ancient world of the New Testament era than many of us have realized. This is one reason I believe the answer to the missional question takes us back to the ancient sources. These early Christians had no authority within their culture for several centuries. This came at a cost to them, and it may well cost us, too, if we regain their perspective.

Many American churches and their leaders have functioned as though the real problem is in our culture. As a result, we have seen a myriad of renewal models that have failed us. I believe the real tragedy is that the culture and the church are now so much alike that it is virtually impossible to tell the difference. Numerous surveys illustrate this point. The spiritual and moral decisions made by Christians and non-Christians are not much different. But there really is a Christian value system, ethical standard, way of devotion, even a Christian attitude about money, ambition, and lifestyle. This true Christian way is at such an obvious variance with the American way that following Christ calls leaders and churches to a whole new paradigm—the one I call missional-ecumenism.

John Stott may have done more for missional-ecumenism than any evangelical in our lifetime. In his magnificent book on the Sermon on the Mount, he sums up my understanding well:

> Too often the church has turned away from this challenge [to live as "God's alternative society"] and sunk into a bourgeois, conformist respectability. At such times it is almost

indistinguishable from the world, it has lost its saltness, its light is extinguished, and it repels all idealists. For it gives no evidence that it is God's new society which is tasting already the joys and powers of the age to come. Only when the Christian community lives by Christ's manifesto [the Sermon on the Mount] will the world be attracted and God be glorified. So when Jesus calls us to himself, it is to this that he calls us. For he is the Lord of the counter-culture.[3]

The culture with its decadence, relativism, consumerism, and wanton rebellion against the revealed will of God is actually the symptom of our problem. The root cause is a deeply divided, morally compromised, theologically indifferent, biblically ignorant, and culturally conformed church. The gospel has been reduced to a minimal set of consumer-related facts. The "sinner's prayer" has replaced the kind of radical conversion that results in life-changing grace. In the process, the larger narrative of creation, fall, redemption, and re-creation has been lost. With this loss there is no coherent understanding of the kingdom of God. The church has now become a religious society of the comfortable. Serious Christians should cry out to God for his mercy and grace to be poured out on the church.

A major paradigm shift is called for if we are to experience reformation and renewal. We need a new way of thinking and living expressed in the missional-ecumenical paradigm. It is time leaders give up trying to mobilize the church to moralize the culture. Political action has its proper place, but it pales in significance to this vision of missional-ecumenism. What is needed is an army of one — an army of men and women who truly love Jesus Christ and live totally "for Christ and his kingdom."[4] Anything less will fail to provide a solution.

THE 80/20 RULE

In any society, organization, or church, approximately 20 percent of the people will lead and bring about change. In general, 80 percent will follow. The 20 percent are activists who will push things forward; the 80 percent are those who become interested in the vision but are followers. The 80 percent must be urged to help the 20 percent accomplish the work, but they will never take responsibility for the vision. This formula has been proven over and over in every social setting. I want to make it clear—there is nothing wrong with being in the 80 percent group. The majority of people are needed to help carry the load. This seems to be the way God wired us.

I have specifically asked God for the 20 percent who will see the vision I have shared and take action. The 80 percent expect us to do it. The 80 percent will always wait for the 20 percent to lead. The 20 percent will usually be the readers and thinkers who make things happen in a church or community—the ones who will engage ideas such as those contained in this book and then act on them decisively. These are the same people who generally know what is going on in the culture and the church. If these leaders do not act, change will not happen. I find pastors often miss this observation, especially when they expect their entire church to grasp their vision. The result is passive Christianity and thousands of churches that lack clear vision. Leaders must lead, and people will follow. This is why the task of equipping leaders is so crucial for the missional-ecumenical vision.

The 80/20 rule is not something I dreamed up. It didn't come from taking a poll. It is a simple, observable social pattern that researchers have discovered. But knowing this rule can help leaders understand what it takes to transform churches.

Consider what this means for you and your church. Are you in the 80 percent or the 20 percent? Your answer cannot be wrong. I am wired to be a 20 percent person. I knew this when I was a young child exploring the woods in Tennessee. Once you know where you fit, you can see your role in addressing the "small church" syndrome that compromises our witness.

WHAT NEXT?

Every Christian should be asking basic questions about this vision of missional-ecumenism. If you are in the 20 percent, you must act if you are convinced. Here are several steps to take.

ASK THE RIGHT QUESTIONS

Somehow Christian leaders stopped asking hard questions. We act as though we already have all the answers, so we hire professionals to tell us how the stock answers work. If a church disagrees with the leaders, in many instances the congregation will find someone else to deliver their message.

Ask this question: What means have proven the most effective for introducing non-Christians to the gospel? (I am not asking what methods will add more members to your congregation.) If you ask this question, you will likely find real answers; if you fail to ask it, very little will happen. You must attempt to move the church toward a missional mind-set, but remember that vision creates friction. Arm yourself with insight and prayer.

I am sure of this: God is a relational being. No program or activity can ever replace relationships. Jesus' life and mission illustrate this powerfully. He took the time to relate to people one-on-one, and we must do the same. Being missional does not mean finding a new program that is better than an old one; being missional means asking, "How can this community of believers become the incarnational expression of the love of Christ in this place?"

MAKE THE KINGDOM CENTRAL

The kingdom of God is central to the mission of the church. We must do everything that we can to show people what this means. Only when people stop thinking of the church as a place to attend and start thinking of the kingdom of God as the sovereign rule of Christ in all of life will they recover a healthy view of the church. The goal of the church should be to create a true counterculture, as John Stott said. We are not offering solutions to people's lives based on market surveys; we are striving to be a congregation that lives under the divine rule.

Every church has a contextualized gospel. We all hear the gospel (the unchangeable truth of the good news) in the culture in which we receive it. We must learn to speak the language of the people we minister to so they can understand the message of Christ. Such contextualization requires us to be careful not to fall into syncretism, where we conform to the patterns of this world (Romans 12:2). But it also means we must not descend into sectarianism, where we elevate our views or the views of our Christian denomination above the gospel. When we fail to keep the kingdom central to mission, we transfer our cultural baggage into the gospel. In the apostle Paul's day, this included items such as meat offered to idols, days of worship, dietary restrictions, and the like (see Acts 10; 15; Romans 14–15; 1 Corinthians 10:14–33). In our day, it includes things such as the day and time we worship, tattoos, plastic surgery, homeschooling, musical styles, Bible translations, the use of language, dress styles, and the like.

If we are to grasp the gospel of the kingdom, we must realize that the Great Commission is not about making converts but about making disciples who can change marriages, families, workplaces, communities, cities, and nations. Discipleship, understood in terms of the present reign of Christ, requires us to value relationships above programs and numbers (Matthew 22:24–40). This vision will require us to teach what we call "worldview" Christianity, but it requires much more than mastering "worldview" content. The goal of equipping a person to be a disciple is real conformity to Christ's pattern of life. This requires new disciplines (from the word *disciple*). Thus, missional-ecumenical leaders must intentionally equip Christians to form lifelong habits that will support the kind of profound changes missional-ecumenism requires.

Jesus taught his disciples to pray, "Your kingdom come, your will be done, on earth as it is in heaven" (Matthew 6:10). If the kingdom of God were to come into your life, family, neighborhood, and workplace, what would it look like? What things would change and why? How might these questions guide your congregation toward a deeper connection with the larger reality of the kingdom of God?

If I were a pastor, I would teach three great biblical truths to the church until I began to see our congregation change:

- the meaning of the kingdom of God and its relationship to the church (Gospels)
- the meaning of the missional church concept and the importance and power of unity (Epistles)
- the meaning of the future glory (nonspeculative and hopeful eschatology) of the people of God as seen in the biblical emphasis on total redemption and vital hope (Epistles and Revelation)

We have been severely damaged by pessi-millennialism, an emphasis on the end of the age that destroys hope rather than creates it. Leaders need to cast a forward look that is saturated with hope and joy. The early church had this perspective, and they changed the world. The church in China has it too. All too often we have looked for signs of the end rather than envisioning what God will do before Christ comes.

CONSIDER THE BLESSING

Please note my use of the word *blessing*, not *blessings*. God promised Abraham that through his descendants the whole world would be blessed (Genesis 12:3). This promise about God blessing the world through Abraham is cited by the apostle Peter in a sermon in Acts 3:25. The entire context of this sermon, which follows a kingdom sign, says that God will bless the whole earth by turning people from their wicked ways to Jesus (Acts 3:26).

This blessing of the covenant is a central biblical concept for understanding the purpose of God and our corporate salvation. But this truth has been distorted into an arbitrary favoritism by a misunderstanding of the biblical truth of election. Lesslie Newbigin correctly grasps the missional understanding of election:

> We cannot know for what *reason* one was chosen, [but] we can most certainly know for what *purpose* he was chosen: he was chosen in order to be a fruit-bearing branch of the one true vine (John 15:16), a witness through whom others might be saved. He is chosen in order that through him God's saving purpose may reach to others, and they too be reconciled to God in and through his reconciled and reconciling people. And while the ultimate mystery of election remains, one can see that the principle of election is the only principle congruous with the nature of God's redemptive purpose.[5]

Every blessing that God has ever poured into our lives is a sovereign gift and a divine stewardship. We are not meant to hoard blessings but to share them generously. The happiest people I know are Christians who are busy sharing the blessing of God. And the most alive congregations I know are doing the same. When we embrace our defining purpose—"the blessing of the world" — and act on it in a corporate way, we become missional people and congregations. And when we share this blessing with other Christians and congregations, we become ecumenical people and congregations.

Ask this question honestly: How is my church a specific blessing to my community? (Recall some of the stories in chapter 18.) How would our neighbors answer this question? Are we a blessing to them, or do we communicate judgment, rejection, anger, and frustration?

CONCLUSION

I am convinced that every reader of this book can do something about this call to missional-ecumenism. You can talk about this vision with other Christians and pray for the kingdom of God to come with power. You can share your love for Christ with your Christian friends who attend other churches. These small efforts will make you a more compassionate Christian, and in the process you will become more like Jesus. Isn't that the point?

But I am convinced that something else needs to happen. People must catch this vision in a powerful way. We must never take no for an answer when it comes to being missional-ecumenical people. Those of us who are in the 20 percent group must take responsibility. Only then will others catch the vision — a vision deeply rooted in Scripture and in the patterns of spiritual renewal that have occurred throughout the entire history of the Christian church.

All of this will require unusual grace and profound sacrifice. Let's be really honest. Most of us give up too easily. Hard work and sacrifice are not what we instinctively want to accept as our calling. This vision requires us to pray and fast. It will require us to surrender our small plans and embrace a bigger vision of the church, no matter what the size of our local congregation may be. Frankly, to do this, you must die. No one likes to think about dying, but there is no other way to pursue this vision. Jesus made this patently clear, and, fittingly so, he has the last word:

> "The hour has come for the Son of Man to be glorified. Very truly I tell you, unless a kernel of wheat falls to the ground

and dies, it remains only a single seed. But if it dies, it pro-
duces many seeds. Those who love their life will lose it, while
those who hate their life in this world will keep it for eternal
life. Whoever serves me must follow me; and where I am,
my servant also will be. My Father will honor the one who
serves me."

John 12:23 – 26

Glossary

Apostolic: That which possesses the sanction and authority of the apostles because of its relationship to their teaching.

Catholic/Catholicity: A transliteration of the Greek word *katholikos*, which means "throughout the whole" or "general." In early church literature, *catholic* referred to the universal church—the whole church diffused throughout the world. *Catholicity* refers to the quality or state of universality, thus bringing to mind the comprehensive nature of the undivided church of Jesus Christ that gathers all of God's people into one church from many different races, languages, and cultures.

Classical Christianity: A way to describe the ancient practices and confessions of the catholic church, both East and West. The word is increasingly used as a way of referring to the importance of tradition in the history of Christianity.

Critical Realism: In philosophy, the theory that some of our sense data accurately represents external objects, proper ties, or events and some sense data does not. Critical realism maintains that there really is an objectively knowable reality, but it must be approached by critical perception. More and more theologians are using the term (for example, T. F. Torrance, John Polkinghorne, Alister McGrath, and N. T. Wright). Wright describes critical realism as "a way of describing the process of 'knowing' that acknowledges the *reality of the thing known, as something other than the knower* (hence 'realism'), while fully acknowledging that the only access we have to this reality lies along the spiraling path of *appropriate dialogue or conversation between the knower and the thing known* (hence 'critical')."[1] We discover Christian truth in a context of dialogue with the truth because we (the knower) must personally relate to the thing known (God's truth) in a relational way.

Didache: An early (second century) anonymous manual of Christian instruction about how to live the life of faith and how to govern the church.

Ecumenical/Ecumenism: From the Greek word *oikoumenē*, which means "the whole inhabited world." Initially used to refer to the early general councils of the church, *ecumenical* has come to refer to Christians and churches scattered geographically and denominationally around the world.

Evangelical: The term means "pertaining to the evangel" — to the good news (gospel). In the Protestant Reformation, it became virtually synonymous with Protestant faith. Following various worldwide renewals and awakenings, the word came to designate Christians who believed that faith, grace, and conversion were essential to the Christian life. It is now often associated with "conservative Protestant."

Gnosticism: A movement in the ancient world that challenged early Christianity by emphasizing a special higher truth that only the enlightened receive from God. It taught that all matter was evil. As a result of these two emphases, it denied the humanity of Jesus.

Great Tradition: The core, elemental truths that are essential to historical and confessional Christianity (for example, the Trinity, the divinity and humanity of Christ, the authority of Scripture, and the like). C. S. Lewis spoke of "mere Christianity," which is his way of saying much the same thing. Christians come from different traditions, but they hold in common the "Great Tradition."

Kerygma: The Greek word meaning "the act of proclaiming" or "the message proclaimed." The *kerygma* is the core message that announces God's decisive act and offer of salvation in the death and resurrection of Jesus Christ (see Romans 16:25; 1 Corinthians 1:21; 15:3 – 5). *Kerygma* precedes detailed teaching, or *didache*.

Lectio divina: The Latin term meaning "divine reading." It also carries the idea of "prayerful reading." The term refers both to the material that a person reads and the act of reading itself. Saint Benedict encouraged the practice, making it a standard part of monastic practice. It is being rediscovered in modern times as a bridge for reading Scripture spiritually.

Logos: A Greek term meaning "word" or "message," *logos* is used in the prologue of John's gospel to refer to the preexistent divine Word (Jesus Christ), who "became flesh and made his dwelling among us." The Old Testament spoke of *logos* as the creative power and personified self-revelation of God (Psalms 33:6, 9; 107:20; Isaiah 55:10–11). In later theology the term came to refer to reason, thus prompting some to equate reason with Christ. At the Council of Nicaea, *logos* was used interchangeably with "Son of God" as the second person of the divine Trinity.

Magisterium: A Latin term meaning "the office of the teacher." In Roman Catholic theology, it refers to the authoritative teaching office of the gospel in the name of Christ, yet as serving and not as superior to the Word of God. All believers are anointed by God and should read and interpret Scripture, but only the magisterium, the whole college of bishops (as successors to the college of apostolic witnesses), united with the bishop of Rome (pope), have final authority.

Missio Dei: The Latin term, meaning "the mission of God," came into prominence in the twentieth century as a way to ground missionary theory and practice in the activity of the triune God. The three persons are involved in "the sending" of the Son into the world and thus the church is "sent" because the sending God reaches out to the world.

Missional: A relatively recent theological term that reconceptualizes the idea inherent in the *missio Dei* (mission of God). It underscores the idea that in sending us into the world as his "sent ones," God has designed that we will carry out his mission in community and action. The key text is John 20:21: "As the Father has sent me, I am sending you." Christopher Wright rightly states, "Mission is and always has been God's before it becomes ours. The whole Bible presents a God of missional activity, from his purposeful, goal-oriented act of creation to the completion of his cosmic mission in the redemption of the whole of creation—a new heaven and a new earth."[2]

Missional-ecumenism: In formulating this term, I have taken two words and put them together as a hyphenated word. I wish to stress these two truths: (1) God is both a unity in himself and as such is a sending God, and (2) God's revealed desire is that we would be (relationally) one with him in this sending and sent (mission) process—thus the term *missional-ecumenism*.

Mystery: Any truth made known to us by divine revelation and believed through faith. Some mysteries in Scripture have been revealed in a way that makes them now more clearly understood than previously. Generally the term has been used to describe a truth not fully comprehended until the age to come (for example, most Christians believe that the sacraments are mysteries).

Mystical: A spiritual truth that is best related to intuitive knowledge and meditation. A mystical experience is one that is related to contemplative union or a state of overwhelming feeling.

Ontological: Formed from the Greek words *ontos* ("of being") and *logia* ("subject under discussion," "study"), *ontology* means "the study of being." The ontology of God is, therefore, his *essential being*.

Orthodox: From the Greek words *orthos* ("correct," "true") and *doxa* ("opinion," "belief," "notion"). The term came into the church at the Council of Chalcedon to express the correct way of understanding divine revelation in Jesus Christ. I am using the term in this way. I also use it to refer to the churches of the Christian East that evolved into local communities after the death of Theodosius (395), when the Roman Empire was divided into East and West. The (Eastern) Orthodox churches, which experienced division with the bishop of Rome in 1054, are in communion with each other and recognize the patriarch of Constantinople as honored among equals.

Orthodoxy: The body of doctrines taught by Scripture, such as the deity and humanity of Christ, the Trinity, and the authority of Holy Scripture. Theologian Thomas C. Oden defines orthodoxy as the "integrated biblical teaching as interpreted in its most consensual classic period."

Paleo-Orthodoxy: From the Greek word *palaios* ("ancient," "long ago") and the word *orthodox* ("correct belief"; see definition of *orthodox* above), *paleo-orthodoxy* (a term coined by the theologian Thomas Oden) refers to the belief that the Christian faith can be found in the consensual beliefs rooted in the ancient sources (dating back especially to the first five centuries of the church).

Papacy: The office of the bishop of Rome, the supreme pontiff of the Roman Catholic Church—the pope.

Patristic(s): The Latin word means "the fathers" or "the study of the fathers." Patristics refers to the theology of the early church theologians (the fathers).

Roman Catholic: A person who is a communicant in the Roman Catholic Church; or pertaining (adjectivally) to the teaching and practice of Roman Catholicism. The term *Roman Catholicism* came into general use in the Protestant Reformation to identify the beliefs and practices of Christians who accepted the pope as the head of the church, as its supreme earthly authority.

Sect: From the Latin *secta* (from *sequi*, "to follow"), *sect* is commonly used to refer to a group that has broken away from a larger religious group and thus holds distinctive views. In this sense, the earliest Christians were a sect of the Jews. The term often refers to a group that breaks away from an older, established church or to those who follow the unique teachings of a leader who has formed a new group.

Sectarianism: Generally refers to a doctrinaire commitment to one's own views or particular group and often resulting in a narrow-minded devotion. Those who disagree are condemned by sectarians, sometimes harshly. Some sectarians disavow all relationship to an established Christian church. A correspondingly negative connotation is found in the synonym *tribalism*.

Spiritual Formation: The ancient Christian concept of shaping the attitudes, beliefs, and practices that form the lives of faithful Christians. The various disciplines of the Christian life (prayer, meditation, Bible reading, fasting, and the like) are used to alter the way we think and live.

Tradition: An ongoing coherent process in which certain core values of a community are advanced through debates with critics from the outside and interpretive refinements from the inside. Tradition is the means by which the church understands its history and collective memory of Jesus Christ.

Recommended Resources

I refer to a number of useful books and resources in the text, and so I have compiled a list of various resources placed into several categories. The list is available at our website (*www.act3online. com*). A number of wonderful websites can be consulted as well. At *www.act3online.com*, in addition to books and websites, you will discover resources such as video presentations, blogs, and chat rooms for talking to others about missional-ecumenism. You will also find other content I have written on various subjects addressed in this book. All of this material is free.

Notes

chapter one

1. Colleen Carroll, *The New Faithful: Why Young Adults Are Embracing Christian Orthodoxy* (Chicago: Loyola University Press, 2002), 3.
2. Julia Duin, *Quitting Church* (Grand Rapids: Baker, 2008), 13. Terry Eastland, who reviewed the book for *The Wall Street Journal* (September 2, 2008, p. A21), suggests that Duin's data is not broad enough and that the decrease in the birthrate has something to do with this trend. He concludes that one can debate her research but the fact is that people are leaving the church.
3. Duin, *Quitting Church*, 149.

chapter two

1. ACT 3: Advancing the Christian Tradition in the Third Millennium. Visit *www.act3online.com* to see the mission and core commitments of ACT 3.

chapter three

1. ACT 3 was previously called Reformation & Revival Ministries. The name was changed in order to better reflect the missional-ecumenism expressed in our mission statement: "ACT 3 is a ministry to equip leaders for unity in Christ's mission. ACT 3 is deeply committed to enabling Christian leaders to exegete both culture and Scripture in order to speak into our present context in ways that are faithful to the missional purposes of God as revealed in Holy Scripture. We do this by teaching leaders how to connect Jesus' prayer for unity (John 17) with his commission to make disciples of all nations (Matthew 28)."
2. The book for which I served as general editor, *Understanding Four Views of the Lord's Supper* (Grand Rapids: Zondervan, 2007), addresses this issue. My introductory chapter lays out my journey on this particular issue. My concluding chapter seeks to narrow the debate to the only two issues that are important enough to

still remain at the center of the differences we hold regarding the Lord's Supper, differences that should not be glossed over, as the book clearly argues.

chapter four

1. Ben Witherington III, *John's Wisdom: A Commentary on the Fourth Gospel* (Louisville: Westminster, 1995), 274.
2. Clyde L. Manschreck, *A History of Christianity in the World* (Englewood Cliffs, N.J.: Prentice Hall, 1974), 20.
3. Warren Angel, *Yes We Can Love One Another! Catholics and Protestants Can Share a Common Faith* (Carlsbad, Calif.: Magnus Press, 1997), 10.
4. Angel, *Yes We Can Love One Another!* 10.

chapter five

1. Francis A. Schaeffer, *The Mark of the Christian* (Downers Grove, Ill.: InterVarsity, 1970), 35.
2. Schaeffer, *Mark of the Christian*, 21.
3. See David Kinnaman and Gabe Lyons, *unChristian: What a New Generation Really Thinks about Christianity ... and Why It Matters* (Grand Rapids: Baker, 2007). This surprise bestseller gathers the insights of some thirty Christians who span a wide array of ages and traditions and explains how modern people, Americans in particular, really see us. Words such as *hypocritical, antihomosexual, sheltered, too political, judgmental,* and the like jump out at the careful reader. This is an important book to read and to use as we try to correct our Christian household. See also Hemant Mehta, *I Sold My Soul on eBay* (Colorado Springs: WaterBrook, 2007). The author, an atheist, describes his experience of a Sunday morning odyssey in a number of evangelical churches in America and offers an eye-opening assessment of how a non-Christian perceives our gospel presentation and some of our leading churches.
4. Hans Küng, *The Church* (New York: Image Books, 1976), 353–54.

chapter six

1. Raymond E. Brown, *The Gospel and Epistles of John: A Concise Commentary* (Collegeville, Minn.: Liturgical Press, 1988), 86.
2. G. W. Bromiley, *The Unity and Disunity of the Church* (Grand Rapids: Eerdmans, 1958), 9.
3. Bromiley, *Unity and Disunity of the Church*, 10.

4. Jürgen Moltmann, *The Church in the Power of the Spirit* (Minneapolis: Fortress, 1993), 34.

5. P. T. Forsyth, *The Church and the Sacraments* (1917; 2nd ed., London: Independent Press, 1947), 39.

6. See Dietrich Bonhoeffer, *Christ the Center* (New York: HarperCollins, 1960), 60–65.

chapter seven

1. I will consider the Apostles' Creed in more detail in the next chapter. The Nicene Creed is the most ecumenical of all the great creeds and adds the fourth mark of the church (apostolic), a mark not found in the earlier Apostles' Creed. The Nicene Creed was used in both the East (without the famous *filioque* phrase) and the West. The word *filioque* means "and from the Son." This expression, which indicated that the Holy Spirit proceeded from *both* the Father and the Son, was accepted in the Latin West and rejected in the Greek East. The *filioque* appears to have been added to the original creed at the Council of Toledo (AD 589). This point of doctrine, which appears to be unimportant to some Protestants who do not bother to understand it, became central to the doctrinal differences between the East and West by the eleventh century. The Apostles' Creed and the Nicene Creed remain the most foundational written statements of faith preserved from the early church.

2. Luke Timothy Johnson, *The Creed: What Christians Believe and Why It Matters* (New York: Doubleday, 2003), 263.

3. Johnson, *The Creed*, 264.

4. United States Conference of Catholic Bishops, "Welcoming the Stranger Among Us: Unity in Diversity" (Washington, D.C.: USCCB Publishing, 2000), 56.

5. Johnson, *The Creed*, 268.

6. Johnson, *The Creed*, 269.

7. Johnson, *The Creed*, 268–69.

8. Johnson, *The Creed*, 269.

9. Francis A. Schaeffer, *The Mark of the Christian* (Downers Grove, Ill.: InterVarsity, 1970), 20.

10. Johnson, *The Creed*, 274.

11. Johnson, *The Creed*, 275.

chapter eight

1. Philip Schaff, *The Creeds of Christendom* (Grand Rapids: Baker, 1983), 1:15.

2. Luke Timothy Johnson, *The Creed* (New York: Doubleday, 2003), 10–11.
3. See David W. Bercot, ed., *A Dictionary of Early Christian Beliefs* (Peabody, Mass.: Hendrickson, 1998). This wonderful volume contains 704 pages dealing with more than 700 topics discussed by the early church fathers.

chapter nine

1. A whole body of material, much of it written by conservative Protestants, argues that the true church can only be found where separation is an essential doctrine and practice of the church. Unity, by this approach, is found through pursuing division as an article of faith. Every small group that broke away from the mainstream church is viewed as pure and holy precisely because it opposed the compromised Catholic or Orthodox Church. One major problem with this approach, and there are numerous problems, is that it ends up identifying this "true" remnant with all kinds of destructive heresies.
2. Stephen Francis Staten, *Was There Unity in the Sub-Apostolic Church? An Investigation of the Tunnel Period* (Wheaton, Ill.: MA thesis, 1996), 129–30.
3. G. W. Bromiley, *The Unity and Disunity of the Church* (Grand Rapids: Eerdmans, 1958), 17.
4. Bromiley, *Unity and Disunity of the Church*, 20.

chapter ten

1. Robert McAfee Brown, *The Spirit of Protestantism* (New York: Oxford, 1961), 24.
2. Philip Schaff, "The Reunion of Christendom," in *The Dawn of Religious Pluralism*, ed. Richard Hughes Seager (LaSalle, Ill.: Open Court, 1993), 101.
3. Rex A. Koivisto, *One Lord, One Faith: A Theology for Cross-Denominational Renewal* (Wheaton, Ill.: Victor, 1993), 14–15.
4. Koivisto, *One Lord, One Faith*, 15.
5. Claes G. Ryn, "How Conservatives Failed 'the Culture,'" *Modern Age* 32 (Winter 1996): 118.
6. John Calvin, *Institutes of the Christian Religion*, ed. John T. McNeill (Philadelphia: Westminster, 1960), 3.2.14, 15 (p. 1:560–61).
7. Calvin, *Institutes*, 3.2.8 (p. 1:552).
8. Lesslie Newbigin, *Proper Confidence: Faith, Doubt, and Certainty in Christian Discipleship* (Grand Rapids: Eerdmans, 1995), 14.

9. Newbigin, *Proper Confidence*, 14.
10. Newbigin, *Proper Confidence*, 14.
11. Newbigin, *Proper Confidence*, 14.
12. Dietrich Bonhoeffer, *The Cost of Discipleship* (New York: Macmillan, 1963), 69.
13. The term *spiritual formation* is relatively new to many evangelical Christians. It is an ancient concept that puts an emphasis "on the improvement of relationship [with God], on the normative (and formative)" growth of the Christian (Evan B. Howard, *The Brazos Introduction to Christian Spirituality* [Grand Rapids: Baker, 2008], 17). A term more common to Roman Catholic tradition and used in the training of priests and people in religious orders, *spiritual formation* is a "rather general term referring to all attempts, means, instructions, and disciplines intended toward deepening of faith and furtherance of spiritual growth. It includes educational endeavors as well as the more intimate and in-depth processes of spiritual direction" (Howard, *Brazos Introduction*, 17). I use the term to describe an emphasis on the means by which we become more like Christ.
14. Cyril, *Catecheses* 18:23, cited in Alister McGrath, *Christian Theology: An Introduction* (Hoboken, N.J.: Wiley-Blackwell, 2006), 155.
15. Luke Timothy Johnson, *The Creed* (New York: Doubleday, 2003), 269.

chapter eleven

1. The new ecumenism's goal is not mere dialogue between traditions as an end in itself, but rather a new coming together through encountering people from every Christian tradition and confession — concrete encounters among those who share a deeply formed Christian orthodoxy and a commitment to the mission of Jesus Christ as central to the church in the world. Besides informal movements for ecumenism, there are a growing number of formal ones as well. These include the World Evangelical Alliance (WEA), which evolved from the older World Evangelical Fellowship (originally the Evangelical Alliance), and the Global Christian Forum (GCF), whose purpose is "to create an open space wherein representatives from a broad range of Christian churches and interchurch organizations, which confess the triune God and Jesus Christ as perfect in his divinity and humanity, can gather to foster mutual respect, to

explore and address together common challenges." It describes its aim as "building bridges where there are none, overcoming prejudices, creating and nurturing new relationships" (see *www .globalchristianforum.org*).

2. World Evangelical Alliance, "About WEA," *www.worldevangelicals. org*.

3. See Christian Churches Together in the USA: *www. christianchurchestogether.org*. The United States Conference of Catholic Bishops made the decision to become a founding participant in this emerging fellowship, a major breakthrough since this is the first official Catholic participation in such an ecumenical fellowship in the United States.

4. Cited in John Allen Jr., "McCain's VP Choice a Woman—and a Post-denominationalist," *National Catholic Reporter* (August 30, 2008), *http://ncronline.org/node/1739*.

5. Eugene H. Peterson, *A Long Obedience in the Same Direction* (Downers Grove, Ill.: InterVarsity, 1980), 169.

6. John Leith, *The Church: A Believing Fellowship* (Atlanta: John Knox, 1981), 21.

7. Dr. Craig R. Higgins, in a lecture, "Attributes of the Church," Westminster Theological Seminary conference on the doctrine of the church (fall 2007).

8. This is a constant challenge for the church. Two great confessions in the twentieth century addressed this problem. The first, the Declaration of Barmen, was written largely by Karl Barth and was agreed on at the Synod of Barmen in 1934. Hitler's National Socialist movement had sought to provide justification for a new kind of Christianity rooted in the German people as a community. In six short paragraphs, this declaration resisted the subordination of the gospel and the church to any political or social movement and stressed the submission of Christians and the church to Jesus Christ alone. The second twentieth-century confession was the Belhar Confession, written in Afrikaans by the Dutch Reformed Mission Church in South Africa in 1986 and later adopted by the Uniting Reformed Church in Southern Africa (1994) when a merged church was created. This confession will likely be adopted as a fourth form of unity in the Reformed Church in America (the oldest continuous denomination in the United States)—the first formal confessional addition to the RCA in over 350 years.

9. Church of Scotland, *The Confession of Faith* (London: T. Nelson and Sons, 1860), 104–5.

10. H. J. Wotherspoon and J. M. Kirkpatrick, *A Manual of Church Doctrine according to the Church of Scotland* (London: Oxford University Press, 1960), 7.

chapter twelve

1. Robert E. Webber, *Who Gets to Narrate the World?* (Downers Grove, Ill.: InterVarsity, 2008), 24.
2. Webber, *Who Gets to Narrate the World?* 26.
3. G. E. Ladd, "The Kingdom of Christ, God, Heaven," in *Evangelical Dictionary of Theology*, ed. Walter A. Elwell (Grand Rapids: Baker 2001), 657.
4. Richard P. McBrien, "What Is 'the Kingdom of God'?" *Catholic Update* (2003), *www.americancatholic.org/Newsletters/CU/ac0980.asp*.
5. Webber, *Who Gets to Narrate the World?* 31.
6. Cardinal Walter Kasper, *Jesus the Christ* (New York: Paulist, 1977), 265.
7. Rembert Weakland, *Faith and the Human Enterprise* (Maryknoll, N.Y.: Orbis, 1992), 37.
8. Ladd, "Kingdom of Christ, God, Heaven," in *Evangelical Dictionary of Theology*, 660.
9. Joseph Cardinal Ratzinger, *The Meaning of Christian Brotherhood* (1960 German ed.; repr., San Francisco: Ignatius, 1993), 87–91.
10. Ratzinger, *Meaning of Christian Brotherhood*, 91.
11. Vatican II, "Decree on Ecumenism: *Unitatis Redintegratio*" (chapter 2, article 8; 1964), *www.vatican.va/archive/hist_councils/ii_vatican_council/documents/vat-ii_decree_19641121_unitatis-redintegratio_en.html*.
12. Vatican II, "Decree on Ecumenism" (chapter 2, article 8).
13. John W. O'Malley, *What Happened at Vatican II?* (Cambridge, Mass.: Harvard University Press, 2008), 195.
14. John T. Ford, *Saint Mary's Press Glossary of Theological Terms* (Winona, Minn.: St. Mary's Press, 2006), 44.
15. Joseph Cardinal Ratzinger, "The Theological Locus of Ecclesial Movements," *Communio* 25 (Fall 1998): 480–81.
16. Abraham Kuyper, "Sphere Sovereignty," in *Abraham Kuyper: A Centennial Reader*, ed. James D. Bratt (Grand Rapids: Eerdmans, 1998), 488.
17. Karl Barth, *Church Dogmatics* (Edinburgh: T&T Clark, 1956), IV:1:643.

chapter thirteen

1. R. P. C. Hanson, "Tradition," in *The Westminster Dictionary of Christian Theology*, eds. Alan Richardson and John Bowden (Philadelphia: Westminster, 1983), 574.

2. Hanson, "Tradition," in *Westminster Dictionary of Christian Theology*, 574.

3. Webber's *A Call to an Ancient Evangelical Future* is the best statement of what I have in mind. You can read the call (and other related papers) at *www.ancientfutureworship.com*. Webber states that ancient/future evangelicalism has three commitments: (1) a faith that returns us to our ancient roots; (2) a faith characterized by connection; and (3) a faith that seeks to be authentic in the changing modern world (see *www.growcenter.org/AnIntroductiontotheAncientFutureMovement.htm.*

4. Béla Vassady, *Christ's Church: Evangelical, Catholic, and Reformed* (Grand Rapids: Eerdmans, 1965), 50.

5. Hanson, "Tradition," in *Westminster Dictionary of Theology*, 576.

6. Allegorical interpretation means a story or portion of Scripture can be interpreted to reveal a deeper or hidden meaning. One of evangelicalism's favorite books, *The Pilgrim's Progress*, is an allegory about the Christian life. It seems odd that we realize we can use this method for nonbiblical literature but then assume the divine intent of the Holy Spirit in Scripture almost never uses this method to feed the soul of the church in a deeper way.

7. I am aware of at least three ongoing evangelical Protestant projects that take readers into the writings of the ancient writers of the church on Holy Scripture: *Ancient Christian Commentary on Scripture* (InterVarsity), a twenty-nine-volume series under the general editorship of Thomas C. Oden; *The Church's Bible* (Eerdmans), under the general editorship of Robert Louis Wilken (providing much longer contextually rich insights from both the early church fathers and medieval commentators); and *Brazos Theological Commentary on the Bible* (Baker), under the general editorship of R. R. Reno, another able student of the early church. I urge all Christians, especially ministers, to use these wonderful volumes. They will change how you hear Scripture and allow you to enter into a catholicity of spirit that is invigorating to both mind and soul.

8. Erik Routley, *The Wisdom of the Fathers* (London: SCM Press, 1957), 9–10.

9. C. S. Lewis, "On the Reading of Old Books," in *God in the Dock* (Grand Rapids: Eerdmans, 1970), 200. First published as the introduction to Saint Athanasius's *The Incarnation of the Word of God* (London: Geofrey Bles, 1944), 200–202.

10. Christopher A. Hall, *Learning Theology from the Church Fathers* (Downers Grove, Ill.: InterVarsity, 2002), 10.

11. Anthony Ugolnik, *The Illuminating Icon* (Grand Rapids: Eerdmans, 1989), 92 (cited by Hall in *Learning Theology from the Church Fathers*, 10.

12. Hanson, "Tradition," in *Westminster Dictionary of Theology*, 576.

13. Alasdair MacIntyre, *Whose Justice? Whose Rationality?* (Notre Dame, Ind.: University of Notre Dame Press, 1988), 12.

14. Vincent of Lerins, *The Commonitories*, in The Fathers of the Church series (Washington, D.C.: Catholic University of America Press, 1970), 270.

15. Thomas Oden, *Requiem: A Lament in Three Movements* (Nashville: Abingdon, 1995), 130.

16. Lewis Sperry Chafer, *Systematic Theology* (Dallas: Dallas Theological Seminary Press, 1948), 8:5–6.

17. In consulting several evangelical books of quotations in writing this book, I found several that listed a number of quotes under the subheading of *Unity*. In many cases they did not provide one positive quotation about unity but only warnings against it.

chapter fourteen

1. See the first three chapters of Paul's first letter to the Corinthians.

2. Lesslie Newbigin, *The Household of God* (London: SCM Press, 1953), 70.

3. Luke Timothy Johnson, *The Creed* (New York: Doubleday, 2003), 263.

4. Newbigin, *Household of God*, 79.

5. Donald Fairbairn, *Eastern Orthodoxy through Western Eyes* (Louisville, Ky.: Westminster, 2002), 23.

6. Anthony Ugolnik, *The Illuminating Icon* (Grand Rapids: Eerdmans, 1989), 264.

7. Ugolnik, *Illuminating Icon*, 266.

8. Johnson, *The Creed*, 263.

9. Johnson, *The Creed*, 264.

10. The ancient term for this is *perichoresis*, which refers to the indwelling, or mutual interpenetration, of the three persons of the Trinity. The term underscores the eternal unity of the three persons in the Trinity.

11. Newbigin, *Household of God*, 76.
12. Newbigin, *Household of God*, 51.
13. Winthrop Hudson, "Denominationalism as a Basis for Ecumenicity," *Church History* 24 (1955): 32 (cited in Rex Koivisto, *One Lord, One Faith* [Wheaton, Ill.: Victor, 1993], 87).
14. See Lesslie Newbigin, *The Reunion of the Church*, rev. ed. (London: SCM Press, 1960), 113. This argument is made in how Newbigin sets the stage for *The Household of God* in his first chapter ("The Setting of the Subject") as well as in chapter 2 ("The Congregation of the Faithful").
15. Geoffrey Wainwright, *Lesslie Newbigin: A Theological Life* (New York: Oxford University Press, 2000), 399. John Paul Todd provides resources on this subject at his excellent website (*www.e4unity.wordpress.com*).

chapter fifteen

1. Keith Hardman, "Christian," in *The New International Dictionary of the Christian Church*, gen. ed., J. D. Douglas, (Grand Rapids: Zondervan, 1978), 220.
2. Mikel Neumann, "Nominal Christian," in *Evangelical Dictionary of World Missions*, gen. ed., A. Scott Moreau, (Grand Rapids: Baker, 2000), 694.
3. *The Orthodox Study Bible* (Nashville: Nelson, 2008), 1535.
4. John Chrysostom, *The Homilies of S. John Chrysostom on the Acts of the Apostles* (Oxford: J. Parker, 1851), 358.

chapter sixteen

1. Daniel L. Migliore, "The Missionary God and the Missionary Church," *Princeton Seminary Bulletin*, 19/1 (Spring 1998): 21.
2. Darrell Guder, ed., *Missional Church: A Vision for the Sending of the Church in North America* (Grand Rapids: Eerdmans, 1998).
3. Vatican II, "Decree on the Mission Activity of the Church" (*Ad Gentes* 2), *www.vatican.va/archive/hist_councils/ii_vatican_council/documents/vat-ii_decree_19651207_ad-gentes_en.html*.
4. Darrell L. Guder, "The Church as Missional Community," in *The Community of the Word*, eds. Mark Husbands and Daniel J. Treier (Downers Grove, Ill.: InterVarsity, 2005), 114. The *Oxford English Dictionary* notes the first recorded use of the word *missional* in 1907 but observes that the term was rarely used until recent years.
5. Lesslie Newbigin, *The Reunion of the Church*, rev. ed. (London: SCM Press, 1960), 100.

6. Lesslie Newbigin, *The Household of God* (London: SCM Press, 1953), 149.

7. Newbigin, *Household of God*, 150.

8. Quoted in David Watson, *I Believe in the Church* (Grand Rapids: Eerdmans, 1978), 337–38.

9. Oliver Tomkins, "John R. Mott," in *The Dictionary of the Ecumenical Movement*, eds. Nicholas Lossky et al. (Grand Rapids: Eerdmans, 1991), 704–5.

10. Tomkins, "John R. Mott," in *Dictionary of the Ecumenical Movement*, 705.

11. The shining exception is seen in the results of the World Evangelical Alliance (see chapter 11).

12. Geoffrey Wainwright, *Lesslie Newbigin: A Theological Life* (New York: Oxford University Press, 2000), 17.

13. Guder, "Church as Missional Community," in *The Community of the Word*, 114.

14. Guder, "Church as Missional Community," in *The Community of the Word*, 116.

15. Darrell Guder, *The Continuing Conversion of the Church* (Grand Rapids: Eerdmans, 2000), 10.

16. Guder, *Continuing Conversion of the Church*, 19.

17. Guder, *Continuing Conversion of the Church*, 20.

18. Guder, *Continuing Conversion of the Church*, 189.

19. Brother Yun, *Living Water* (Grand Rapids: Zondervan, 2008), 141.

20. This point is well stated by Glenn Wagner in an essay titled "Biblical Unity and Biblical Truth: A Necessary Tension," in *Seven Promises of a Promise Keeper*, eds. Bill McCartney, Greg Laurie, and Jack Hayford (Nashville: Nelson, 1999), first published as a pamphlet by Promise Keepers in 1997 to explain its practices with regard to its interdenominational witness. I have gained several helpful ideas from this simple but extremely thoughtful piece.

chapter seventeen

1. Joseph Bottum, "The Death of Protestant America," *First Things* 185, (August/September 2008): 23–33.

2. Language such as this is used in the second paragraph of *Ut Unum Sint* (That They May Be One), Pope John Paul II's encyclical on ecumenism (May 25, 1995), *www.vatican.va/holy_father/ john_paul_ii/encyclicals/documents/hf_jp-ii_enc_25051995_ ut-unum-sint_en.html*.

3. Vatican II, "Decree on Ecumenism: *Unitatis Redintegratio*" (chapter 2, article 8; 1964), *www.vatican.va/archive/hist_councils/ ii_vatican_council/documents/vat-ii_decree_19641121_unitatis-redintegratio_en.html.*

4. James I. Packer, *Taking Christian Unity Seriously* (Milton, Ont., Canada: Anglican Essentials Canada, 2007), 5.

5. Packer, *Taking Christian Unity Seriously,* 5.

6. Packer, *Taking Christian Unity Seriously,* 5–6.

7. Packer, *Taking Christian Unity Seriously,* 6.

8. Packer, *Taking Christian Unity Seriously,* 6.

9. Packer, *Taking Christian Unity Seriously,* 7.

10. Quoted in *Ut Unum Sint* (That They May Be One), Pope John Paul II's encyclical on ecumenism (May 25, 1995), section 20, *www .vatican.va/holy_father/john_paul_ii/encyclicals/documents/hf_ jp-ii_enc_25051995_ut-unum-sint_en.html.*

11. David Watson, *I Believe in the Church* (Grand Rapids: Eerdmans, 1978), 346.

12. Vatican II, "Dogmatic Constitution on the Church: *Lumen Gentium*" (chapter 2, article 12), *www.vatican.va/archive/hist_ councils/ii_vatican_council/documents/vat-ii_const_19641121_ lumen-gentium_en.html.*

13. Quoted in Watson, *I Believe in the Church,* 347.

14. Watson, *I Believe in the Church,* 347.

chapter eighteen

1. At *www.act3online.com* you can share stories and leave testimonies for others to read and be encouraged. Look for the feature connected to *Your Church Is Too Small.*

2. Hugh Halter and Matt Smay, *The Tangible Kingdom: Creating Incarnational Community* (San Francisco: Jossey-Bass, 2008).

3. At *www.act3oneline.com* you can learn about our equipping ministry for helping leaders understand how to put this truth into practice. Many other organizations offer similar training. The important thing is that you get the help you need.

4. A list of churches and information about the prayer walk and other related items of mission can be found at *www. streamwoodchurches.com.* The hope is to see a movement of mission reaching into the whole town through the witness of all the churches serving as one.

5. Quoted in *Ut Unum Sint* (That They May Be One), Pope John Paul II's encyclical on ecumenism (May 25, 1995), sections 22, 23,

*www.vatican.va/holy_father/john_paul_ii/encyclicals/documents/
hf_jp-ii_enc_25051995_ut-unum-sint_en.html.*

6. The Taizé Community, "A Pilgrimage of Trust on Earth," *www.taize
.fr/en_article58.html.*

7. Jason Brian Santos, *A Community Called Taizé: A Story of Prayer,
Worship and Reconciliation* (Downers Grove, Ill.: InterVarsity,
2008).

8. Colson is quoted as stating, "When all is said and done, and
my life is viewed in perspective, ECT is likely to be the most
significant project I invested my time and capital into. It has
been well worth the struggle, and I think we have yet to see the
great things God will do with it" (Jonathan Aitken, *Charles W.
Colson: A Life Redeemed* [Colorado Springs: WaterBrook, 2005],
388). Aitken says that as a result of Colson's ECT commitment,
Prison Fellowship lost $1.5 million. Radio stations dropped the
daily Breakpoint broadcasts, and all over the Bible Belt churches
and pastors protested against PF. Aitken refers to the response
to Colson as "evangelical hostility" — a description I know to
be apt, since I was in the middle of the response and also in
conversation with Colson following the first wave of attacks. His
gracious response to opposition and his genuine love for Christian unity endeared him to me as a strong role model. I gladly
acknowledge my debt to him.

chapter nineteen

1. Catechism of the Catholic Church, "The Church Is One, Holy,
Catholic, and Apostolic," *www.vatican.va/archive/catechism/
p123a9p3.htm.*

2. In a letter from John Calvin to Thomas Cranmer, letter no. 1619,
Calvini Opera 14.313.

3. John R. W. Stott, *The Message of the Sermon on the Mount: Christian Counter-Culture* (Downers Grove, Ill.: InterVarsity, 1978), 222.

4. "For Christ and His Kingdom" is the college motto of my alma
mater, Wheaton College. It came out of an era of great hope and
optimism in the nineteenth century, a time when many Christians
were laboring at great personal sacrifice to end slavery as an evil
curse on American society. I ponder this motto almost daily since
I see it many times a week.

5. Lesslie Newbigin, *The Household of God* (London: SCM Press,
1953), 101.

glossary

1. N. T. Wright, *The New Testament and the People of God* (Minneapolis: Fortress, 1992), 35.
2. Christopher Wright, "An Upside-Down World," *Christianity Today* 51 (January 2007): 45.

ACT 3 is a ministry to equip leaders for unity in Christ's mission.

ACT 3 is deeply committed to enabling Christian leaders to exegete both culture and Scripture in order to speak into our present context in ways that are faithful to the missional purposes of God as revealed in Holy Scripture. We do this by teaching leaders how to connect Jesus' prayer for unity (John 17) with his commission to make disciples of all nations (Matthew 28).

We express this purpose through four core convictions:

Missional Character of the Church

We believe that the life and witness of the church should be thoroughly shaped by its participation in the mission of God to reconcile the world to himself in Jesus Christ, and by the call of Jesus to be the people of God sent into the world to proclaim and live out the gospel.

Primacy of Scripture

We believe that Scripture is inspired by God and as such is infallible and authoritative for the life and witness of the church throughout history and across cultures.

Indispensable Significance of the Christian Tradition

We affirm the summary of Christian faith taught in the Apostles' Creed and the Nicene Creed and are committed to seeking wisdom from the history and traditions of the one holy catholic and apostolic church.

Necessity of Cultural Engagement

We are committed to ongoing engagement with culture and the world for the sake of our unified witness to the gospel and continual learning from Christians in other cultural settings.

P. O. Box 88216 • Carol Stream, Illinois 601888
www.act3online.com • www.johnharmstrong.com

Understanding Four Views on Baptism

John H. Armstrong, General Editor;
Paul E. Engle, Series Editor

What is the significance of water baptism?
Who should be baptized? Is infant baptism
scriptural? Which is the proper baptismal
mode: sprinkling, pouring, or immersion?
Should people be rebaptized if they join a
church that teaches a different form of baptism? Should baptism be
required for church membership? These and other questions are
explored in this thought-provoking book, edited by John Armstrong.
Four historic views on baptism are considered in depth:

- Baptism of the professing regenerate by immersion (Baptist)
- Infant baptism of children of the covenant (Reformed)
- Infant baptism by sprinkling as a regenerative act (Lutheran)
- Believers' baptism on the occasion of regeneration by
  immersion (Christian Churches/ Churches of Christ)

All contributors use Scripture to present their views, and each responds to the others' essays. This book helps readers arrive at their
own conclusions. It includes resources such as a list of statements
on baptism from creeds and confessions, a list of books on baptism,
and discussion questions for each chapter to facilitate small group
and classroom use.

Softcover: 978-0-310-26267-1

Pick up a copy at your favorite bookstore or online!

Understanding Four Views on the Lord's Supper

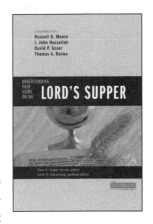

John H. Armstrong, General Editor;
Paul E. Engle, Series Editor

Who should participate in the Lord's Supper? How frequently should we observe it? What does this meal mean? What happens when we eat the bread and drink from the cup? What do Christians disagree about and what do they hold in common? These and other questions are explored in this succinct, challenging book, edited by John Armstrong.

This volume in the Counterpoints: Church Life series allows four contributors to make a case for the following views:

- Baptist view (memorialism)
- Reformed view (spiritual presence)
- Lutheran view (consubstantiation)
- Roman Catholic view (transubstantiation)

All contributors use Scripture to present their views, and each responds to the others' essays. This book helps readers arrive at their own conclusions. It includes resources such as a listing of statements on the Lord's Supper from creeds and confessions, quotations from noted Christians, a list of books on the Lord's Supper, and discussion questions for each chapter to facilitate small group and classroom use.

Softcover: 978-0-310-26268-8

Pick up a copy at your favorite bookstore or online!

Share Your Thoughts

With the Author: Your comments will be forwarded to the author when you send them to *zauthor@zondervan.com*.

With Zondervan: Submit your review of this book by writing to *zreview@zondervan.com*.

Free Online Resources at
www.zondervan.com

Zondervan AuthorTracker: Be notified whenever your favorite authors publish new books, go on tour, or post an update about what's happening in their lives.

Daily Bible Verses and Devotions: Enrich your life with daily Bible verses or devotions that help you start every morning focused on God.

Free Email Publications: Sign up for newsletters on fiction, Christian living, church ministry, parenting, and more.

Zondervan Bible Search: Find and compare Bible passages in a variety of translations at www.zondervanbiblesearch.com.

Other Benefits: Register yourself to receive online benefits like coupons and special offers, or to participate in research.

ZONDERVAN®
.com